Foundation Themes

Homes

Clare Beswick

Credits

British Library Cataloguing-in-Publication Data A catalogue record for this book is available from the British Library.

ISBN 0-439-98465-3

Author
Clare Beswick

Editor
Saveria Mezzana

Assistant Editor
Lesley Sudlow

Series Designer
Joy Monkhouse

Designer
Micky Pledge

Illustrations
Debbie Clark

Cover photography
© Thinkstock

Acknowledgements

The publishers gratefully acknowledge permission to reproduce the following copyright material:

Qualifications and Curriculum Authority for the use of extracts from the QCA/DfEE document *Curriculum Guidance for the Foundation Stage* © 2000 Qualifications and Curriculum Authority

Brenda Williams for 'Click, click, click', 'Friends and neighbours', 'A house of patterns', 'Spider, spider, spins all day', 'House doors', 'Ouch! It's hot!' © 2003, Brenda Williams, all previously unpublished (2003, ©Scholastic Ltd).

Sanchia Sewell for 'My Wheelbarrow', 'The postie's bag', 'Kitchen song', 'I wake up at seven o'clock', 'See that tall building', 'When I'm going up (down) the stairs' © 2003, Sanchia Sewell, all previously unpublished (2003 Scholastic Ltd).

Every effort has been made to trace copyright holders and the publishers apologise for any inadvertent omissions.

Text © 2003 Clare Beswick
© 2003 Scholastic Ltd

Designed using Adobe InDesign

Published by Scholastic Ltd
Villiers House
Clarendon Avenue
Leamington Spa
Warwickshire CV32 5PR

Visit our website at www.scholastic.co.uk

Printed by Belmont Press

1 2 3 4 5 6 7 8 9 0   3 4 5 6 7 8 9 0 1 2

Contents

Chapter 1
My home

Chapter 3
My home, my street

Chapter 2
Inside my home

Chapter 4
Animal homes

Contents

Chapter 5

Unusual homes

Circle time

Displays

Photocopiables

Rhymes

Songs

Activities

Foundation Themes

Homes

Introduction

Home is the very centre of the universe for young children, and their learning grows from the security and warmth of home. Their play and first interests centre around home and the familiar routines and objects found in it. Gradually, their interests expand to include their neighbourhood and the homes of those around them, their friends and their community. As each child's confidence grows, their natural curiosity drives them to learn more about the world around them. This book on the theme of 'Homes' focuses not just on a child's own home, but on homes in their neighbourhood, and also includes more unusual homes, as well as animal homes, to build knowledge and understanding of their world. It contains fun, practical activities that are clearly linked to the Stepping Stones and Early Learning Goals, as detailed in the QCA document *Curriculum Guidance for the Foundation Stage*. These activities cover all six Areas of Learning and provide a wealth of original and innovative ideas to develop children's learning and experiences through the theme of 'Homes'.

The ideas suggested can be applied equally well to the documents on pre-school education published for Scotland, Northern Ireland and Wales. The activities are suitable for use in all early years settings, and only readily available materials and resources are needed to complete them.

Personal, social and emotional development

Communication, language and literacy

Mathematical development

Knowledge and understanding of the world

Physical development

Creative development

© Derek Cooknell

Using this book

All of the activities are accessible to all children in the Foundation Stage, from those just embarking on the Foundation Stage to Reception year children who are close to achieving the expected goals. Many of the activities are for small groups of up to four children. Whole-group activities are also included, with many ideas readily adaptable to different-sized groups, according to the needs of the children and to the size of your group.

The activity pages are divided into five chapters:
♦ My home
♦ Inside my home
♦ My home, my street
♦ Animal homes
♦ Unusual homes.

For each activity, the Stepping Stone and Early Learning Goal are listed, with a logo indicating which Area of Learning the activity relates to (see logos in left panel). The Stepping Stones are colour-coded, to show whether the activity is at the simplest level (yellow), at a higher level (blue) or at the highest level (green),

Foundation Themes
Homes

to match the colours used to show progression in the QCA document *Curriculum Guidance for the Foundation Stage*. On each page, the group size, resources needed and any preparation required are also described, and clear, concise step-by-step instructions take you through the activity.

Each activity page includes additional support ideas to ensure that the activity is accessible to the youngest children and to the children who are working at an early developmental level. Ideas are also included to extend the activities for children developing skills beyond the Early Learning Goals.

Links with the children's parents or carers and families are essential and a part of everyday good practice in early years settings, therefore, every activity page offers ideas to promote and develop links between the setting and the children's homes, under the heading 'Home partnership'.

Across the book, there is a whole range of further ideas that offer endless opportunities to extend the theme, follow the children's particular interests and provide for further practice of essential skills. The 'Further ideas' section on each page suggests two or three extra activities to carry out with the children.

© Derek Cooknell

Circle time is now a regular feature in many early years settings. It is a chance for the children to build their self-confidence and self-esteem, and to develop their speaking, listening and thinking skills. Ideas for circle time activities are provided using the same clear, step-by-step approach as on the activity pages.

This books also presents ideas for displays around the theme of 'Homes'. All the displays are interactive, collaborative and focused on the children's own work, and offer a range of additional learning opportunities. Suggestions on how the display can be used are also listed.

The photocopiable pages and the previously unpublished songs and rhymes at the back of the book will help you to provide a new and original spin to this popular early years theme.

Using the theme
Many early years settings use a theme to link activities across all Areas of Learning, providing inspiration and focus to all involved – children, parents, carers and staff. Such a cross-curricular approach ensures that children can develop a wide range of concepts, skills and attitudes through a wealth of developmentally appropriate experiences. This book offers a cross-curricular planner on pages 10 and 11 for the theme of 'Homes', which gives a clear, easily interpreted overview of planning for the topic.

The activities in this book have been arranged so that you can plan a whole 'Homes' project, or use some of them in a mini topic, such as 'Animal homes'. Some could also be used as links to other themes, such as 'All about me'. The activities reflect the way that young children learn and their need for very practical, hands-on learning. They also take account of attention and listening skills of children in the Foundation Stage, providing stimulating and visually appealing activities to maximise their concentration span.

Foundation Themes
Homes

Planning

Effective planning ensures that all children have a rich blend of experiences and opportunities that enable them to work towards the Early Learning Goals. A theme such as 'Homes' provides a useful focus for activities and offers excellent motivation and progression for children, parents, carers and staff. Productive plans will help you to ensure the necessary breadth of activities and a range appropriate to a variety of learning styles and developmental levels, and that there is clarity and common understanding about objectives.

Effective planning

Planning can take many different forms, and while there is no set format, it is helpful to consider the common features of effective planning. Plans need to be practical, concise working documents. They need to be devised by staff working together, referred to frequently and displayed for parents and carers. They provide the framework for all children's learning. The most effective plans:

♦ are rooted in a clear knowledge of the children's experiences, skills, needs, interests and learning styles

♦ identify the purpose of activities clearly, outlining what the children will be learning from the activities

♦ show how the activities can be adapted to support children working at different levels and speeds as well as those with special educational needs

♦ outline what the children should do, group sizes and staffing arrangements, and list the resources required.

    When drawing up plans, you need to leave room for spontaneity. This will enable you and your staff to respond flexibly to the needs and interests of the children, building on natural curiosity and emerging special interests. Three levels or layers of planning are needed: long term, medium term and short term.

Long-term plans

The long-term plan is the map of all the experiences that will be offered to the children in the early years. Long-term plans often cover a whole year. Sometimes also known as curriculum maps or frameworks, the long-term plans include the policies and aims of your setting. It should also incorporate national requirements and guidance on the early years, as well as local guidance provided by the Early Years Development and Childcare Partnership. It defines the main objectives and outcomes for learning, covering all six Areas of Learning, and ensures that a breadth and balance of opportunities is offered to the children to prepare them for Key Stage 1 of the National Curriculum. The long-term plan may cover a whole year, but the learning experiences should be divided into manageable blocks, which will be covered in your medium-term planning.

Medium-term plans

The medium-term plan usually covers a term or half-term and is often based around a theme or series of related mini topics. The 'Homes' theme in this book provides the basis for a medium-term plan. The cross-curricular planner on pages 10 and 11 shows how the activities cover all the Areas of Learning.

When preparing your medium-term plans, try to choose a range of themes as vehicles for the children's learning, thinking of the interests of the children, your community and neighbourhood. Include themes that are wide enough to plan an array of relevant, but varied, activities that will engage all the children, be appealing, maintain interest and provide motivation. Consider how seasonal mini topics can be incorporated into wider themes. For example, if the theme for January and February is 'Food', try to think of a way to integrate an 'Ice and snow' mini topic into it. In this book, the activities can be used as 'Homes' mini topics, such as 'Inside my home', 'Unusual homes' and so on.

The medium-term plan lists all the activities to be provided and includes all the learning objectives for the children, specifying what they will know or understand, and what skills they will have gained or refined through the range of experiences. The activities should provide practical hands-on learning, with time and opportunity for the children to make their own discoveries and develop and practise new skills.

© David Mager via Soda

© Ana Esperanza Nance via Soda

A clear, concise medium-term plan ensures that all the team members have a common understanding of what has to be achieved. Agreement needs to be gained on how the effectiveness of the medium-term plans can be evaluated as well as how the children's learning can be assessed against the learning objectives included in the plan. Assessment and evaluation should therefore be incorporated into it, alongside the actual planning of learning objectives and activities.

It is usual at this stage to brainstorm the theme, putting down as many activities and experiences as possible related to the theme. This is a useful exercise, but it is very important to remember that the learning objectives should come first – that is, the activities and experiences should be planned to meet the learning objectives. Devise a theme that is led by what you want the children to have experienced, practised or learned, rather than by the range of activities that you want to provide.

Short-term plans
The short-term plans usually cover one week and include a day-by-day breakdown of learning objectives and activities to be offered. It needs to deal with all the practical matters, such as details of the resources needed, the group size, staffing arrangements and so on. The learning objectives can be broken down into small measurable goals designed to meet the needs of that particular group of children. The short-term plans, while being detailed, need to retain an element of flexibility. This will allow you to make the most of the spontaneity and natural curiosity of the children. The short-term plans also need to specify how assessment will take place and how the activity will be evaluated. For more information about assessment, see pages 13 and 14.

Using this book in planning
Including a 'Homes' theme in your long-term plan provides an opportunity to plan a whole range of activities and experiences focused around the routines, objects and environment most familiar to children. This fits well with the learning style and interests of young children. The theme is also wide enough to allow you to plan learning objectives for children at all developmental levels within the Foundation Stage. It will need to be included in the long-term plans, alongside the more general aims and policies of your setting.

In the medium-term planning, it is often helpful to first consider your main priorities for learning, reflect on the current interests of the children and take into account the range of learning styles that you have observed. Next, with all this in mind, brainstorm the theme, selecting from the activity pages the activities and experiences that are most suited to your setting. Do not forget to look at the further ideas. A blend of the step-by-step activities and the further ideas may be the most appropriate way to meet the needs of the children in your setting. Be confident

Remember that effective planning has three layers (long, medium and short term) and is:
♦ clear, concise and detailed
♦ a working document
♦ devised with colleagues
♦ available to parents and carers
♦ specifies learning objectives
♦ includes assessment and evaluation.

Personal, social and emotional development

ELG Clusters	Activity	Page
Dispositions and attitudes	Warm and safe Our homes If I lived here	16 40 64
Self-confidence and self-esteem	Mr Bear Rainbow colours Around the world	15 28 63
Making relationships	Pizza houses	39
Behaviour and self-control	My pet's home Ssh, be gentle	52 78
Sense of community	Patchwork homes I live in the sea	27 51

Creative development

ELG Clusters	Activity	Page
Exploring media and materials	My front door My treasure bag Tiles and bricks My street	25 38 49 80
Music	Rhythm and rhyme Lights in the house Dolphin music	26 50 62
Imagination	The bears' house Watch out, little piggy!	37 74
Responding to experiences, and expressing and communicating ideas	Safe in my cocoon I live above a shop	61 73

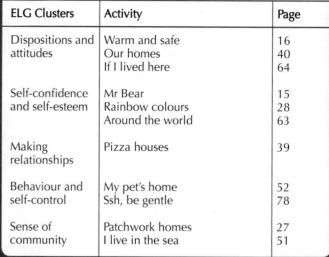

Th F

Ho

Physical development

ELG Clusters	Activity	Page
Movement	Build a wall Threading fun We all put on shoes Going on a journey In a burrow Jump aboard my caravan	23 24 36 47 60 72
Sense of space	Living farm	71
Health and bodily awareness	Sleeping, eating and having fun!	35
Using equipment	Where do I live?	60
Using tools and materials	This is our town Stairs and lifts	48 82

Communication, language and literacy

Mathematical development

Knowledge and understanding of the world

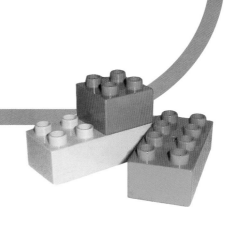

that you know your children best. Select activities that will motivate, challenge and stimulate them. When you have finished brainstorming the theme, look at the ideas and check that they cover all the Areas of Learning, provide opportunities for children at all stages of working towards the Early Learning Goals, and offer a range of learning experiences, both adult-directed and child-led. Remember that it is important to provide a breadth and balance of activities and experiences. Set out your medium-term plans clearly so that all the staff members have a common understanding of what the children should learn through each 'Homes' activity. Use the circle time and display activities to complement your planning, making sure that they are an integral part of your medium-term plan and that their purpose is clear.

Much of the information that you will need to include in your weekly, short-term plans for the 'Homes' activities can be found on the activity pages of this book. The cross-curricular planner on pages 10 and 11 shows the spread of cover among the six Areas of Learning and provides details of which clusters of Early Learning Goals are covered by each of the activities. This enables you to plan a theme on 'Homes', knowing that it will help to deliver the whole Foundation Stage curriculum in an interesting and focused way. Further new resources, such as rhymes, poems and photocopiable activity sheets, can be found at the back of this book. These will supplement the resources that you already have. Try to personalise each activity to your setting and to the specific needs of your children. This will make the activity more meaningful for all concerned, more effective and more of an integral part of the core of activities that you provide on a daily basis.

Equal opportunities

Equality of opportunity needs careful consideration throughout the planning process. It is essential that every aspect of what is provided promotes equality and positive images of all people, and allows all the children equal access to the experiences and activities offered. It is important to reflect the rich mix of cultures that exists in British society, and a theme such as 'Homes' is ideal for this. Avoid making any assumptions about where or how families live. It is important to ensure that the children develop a respect for all communities and the choices that individuals make about their lifestyle and homes.

Look through the resources used and carefully consider how they reflect our multicultural society. Ensure that details are included in the plans of how the activities and experiences will meet the needs of children with special educational needs, listing any additional resources that are required. Check that you have planned how you are going to meet the needs of the youngest children in your group, who may be just starting out in the Foundation Stage and be working around the earliest Stepping Stones, as well as how to challenge the children who are close to, or achieving, the Early Learning Goals.

Assessment

Monitoring children's progress is a key part of the work of the early years practitioner. Assessing, progressing and recording each child's achievements are essential to:

♦ celebrate their successes
♦ monitor progress
♦ identify their strengths and weaknesses
♦ find out about their learning styles
♦ inform planning.

Assessment is an essential part of planning, teaching and learning – it is central to everything that you do in the early years setting. It may be defined as making a decision about whether a child can or cannot do something, is refining a particular skill or using it more frequently, spontaneously or with more confidence, or about whether the skill or attitude in question is emerging.

It is relatively easy to make an effective assessment when the learning objective is clear, such as 'The child can cut along a 10cm straight line', or 'The child recognises numbers 1 to 10', but it is much more difficult if the objective is fuzzy or unclear, such as 'The child understands the differences between shapes'. This fuzzy objective would be much clearer if it mentioned the identification of a circle, square, rectangle and triangle, and the description of a shape by its number of sides and corners, for example. With clear objectives, all practitioners will have a common understanding of what is required, thereby avoiding doubt and uncertainty.

Making clear learning objectives in medium- and short-term planning is the first step towards really effective assessment. However, it is also very important to collaborate on assessment. This means that all staff members have to share information about the children, so that a full and accurate picture of each child's progress is gained. This will also ensure that valuable information about a child's learning style, learning objectives and emerging skills is known to all the staff in the setting.

© Derek Cooknell

Links with home

Parents and carers are important partners in assessment. Not only do practitioners need to share information with them about their children's progress, but parents and carers can also provide valuable information and insight into their children's achievements at home. This sharing of information between home and your setting promotes a healthy partnership, and ensures that practitioners and parents are working together in the children's best interests to assist their learning. You need to plan for formal meetings to share information about progress with parents, as well as provide ample opportunity and the right atmosphere of trust and partnership, to encourage parents to approach you informally to discuss their children's needs.

Foundation Themes
Homes

Collecting evidence

Assessment is a continuous process in the early years, but recording and collecting evidence of children's progress requires planning and organisation. The methods used need to be:
♦ practical
♦ concise
♦ consistent
♦ flexible
♦ clear and unambiguous.
There are three main types of assessment process:
♦ spontaneous records or continuous assessment
♦ planned observation
♦ reflective comments.

Continuous assessment occurs as practitioners naturally observe and work alongside the children on a day-by-day basis. If they record or note down spontaneous observations of new skills, new concepts understood, achievements, comments about the learning needs and styles of individual children, then gradually, a snapshot of each child's progress is gained. In addition, in the child's final term of the Foundation Stage, the staff will be completing individual Foundation Stage Profile documents, recording the progress that the child has made.

On occasions, it is necessary to set up a planned but informal assessment task, activity or observation. This sort of focused assessment will provide opportunity for the practitioner to further observe individual children's progress, as well as to check that skills observed at specific moments in time are a true reflection of each child's achievements. These focused assessments need careful planning and should be included in the medium- and short-term plans. Such planned assessment activities and observations are a good opportunity for the practitioner to listen to the child, observe their attitudes and approaches to other children and reflect on their learning style.

The third strand to effective assessment is stepping back and reflecting on the developmental progress of individual children, recording your own thoughts and observations as well as discussing each child's progress with colleagues. This should be done regularly and in a planned way, perhaps on a half-termly or termly basis.

Records of achievement, folders with examples of the children's work, photographs of displays and so on, are a useful addition to the assessment process and are an important way of celebrating with parents and carers their children's success and achievements.

Finally, the importance of assessment is not confined to monitoring the developmental progress of individual children. Assessment contributes to an overview or evaluation of how effective the activities and experiences provided have been in helping all the children to move towards the Early Learning Goals. Use the outcomes of assessment to inform your planning, identify strengths and weaknesses in your provision and celebrate the strengths of the setting as a whole.

Chapter 1

My home

This chapter provides a range of fun learning activities focused on the children's own homes. It explores the buildings, their location and the importance of home, and it introduces the concept of safety at home.

Mr Bear

Group size
Four to six children.

What you need
The story-book *Peace at Last* by Jill Murphy (Macmillan Children's Books); props such as three bears, clock, car, cup, saucer and envelope; sheet of A3 card; scissors; pens; sheet of A3 paper; glue; sheet of A5 paper for each child.

Preparation
Cut a house shape from the sheet of A3 card and mark out the windows and a door. Fold the sheets of A5 paper in half.

What to do
Introduce the story-book, looking at the front cover and title page. Read slowly to the children, using props to focus on key parts of the story. Re-read the book, showing each page to the children. Talk about how Mr Bear might have felt and why. Discuss how we know how Mr Bear was feeling. Focus on Mr Bear's home and how Mr Bear wanted to feel warm and safe at home. Make a list on a blank sheet of A3 paper of what Mr Bear was doing at home, such as having tea, reading and going to bed. Invite the children to tell you what they like about their own homes. Talk about what makes us feel warm and safe at home.

Give each child a folded sheet of A5 paper and let them choose a favourite story-book character to draw on the inside. Then help them to copy or write their name on the front of their folded picture. Glue all the pictures as windows and a door to the large cut-out of Mr Bear's house.

Place the house, story-book and props in the book corner for the children to enjoy and share later.

Stepping Stone
Express needs and feelings in appropriate ways.

Early Learning Goal
Have a developing awareness of their own needs, views and feelings.

Support and extension
Read the story to a group of two or three younger children and talk about bedtime in their own homes. Ask older children to add words to their pictures.

Home partnership
Encourage parents and carers to share the book, pictures and props with their children. Ask them to talk to their children about bedtime routines and how these have changed as they have grown from babies to small children.

Further ideas
♦ Make a copy of the photocopiable sheet 'Paper house' on page 89 for each child and help them to make a folded paper house. Cut out both templates, colour and make collages on each side of the house, then fold it along the dotted lines and glue the house together as shown, paint the roof template. When the roof is dry, fold it along the dotted line and fix it to the top of the house with sticky tape.
♦ Let the children use recyclable materials to make a models of their bedrooms.

Theme links
All about me
Toys

Warm and safe

Stepping Stone
Display high levels of
involvement in activities.

Early Learning Goal
Be confident to try new
activities, initiate ideas and
speak in a familiar group.

Group size
Up to six children.

What you need
A large sheet of
paper; marker
pen; corrugated
card; balsa wood;
shoeboxes; collage
materials; scissors;
glue; mail-order
catalogues; props
such as a blanket,
heater, safety gate,
key and picture of
a smoke alarm.

What to do
Talk with the children about things
that we use at home to keep us warm
and safe. Discuss each room in the home, in turn, and make a list on the sheet
of paper of different ways in which we keep warm and safe. Invite each child to
choose a prop and say how it could be used. Ask the children to think of other items
that keep us warm and safe.

Encourage the children to carefully cut items from the catalogues that keep
us safe and warm at home. Help the children to glue the corrugated card, boxes
and balsa wood together to build a simple house. Make labels for each room, for
example, write the word 'kitchen' and draw a pan next to it. Invite the children to
fill each room with items cut from the catalogues, focusing on products that keep us
safe and warm, then let them decorate the house with collage materials.

Folded corrugated card

dividers

Lolly-stick window
frames

Balsa-wood room

Shoebox laid on its side

Support and extension
For younger children, look at pictures of kitchen products and talk about how
parents keep children safe in the kitchen. Talk about items that are hot, sharp or
electrical. Ask older children to think about young babies and what we need to do
to keep them warm and safe.

Home partnership
Ask a parent to bath their baby at your setting. Talk to the children about what the
parent is using and how they are making sure that the baby stays safe and warm.
With permission, take photographs of what the parent is using and of the different
parts of the process, such as getting the baby undressed.

Further ideas
♦ Read and talk about the home-safety rhyme 'Ouch! It's hot!' on the
photocopiable sheet on page 83.
♦ Add home-safety products to the home corner, such as oven gloves, a knife
block, bath mat, pretend safety gate, high chair with Velcro harness, pretend smoke
alarm and so on.

Theme links
Babies
Safety

This is my home

Stepping Stone
Use writing as a means of recording and communicating.

Early Learning Goal
Write their own names and other things such as labels and captions.

Group size
Four to six children.

What you need
A copy of the photocopiable sheet 'Zigzag book' on page 90 for each child; coloured backing paper (cut slightly larger than the zigzag-book template) to back each zigzag book; glue; sticky tape; scissors; pens; pencils; name cards; mail-order catalogues; paper and fabric collage materials; photographs of houses; books showing pictures of houses.

Preparation
Cut out the zigzag-book templates and fold them along the dotted lines. Make sure that you know the street name and number for each child's home.

What to do
Look at the photographs and pictures of houses with the children. Talk about common features, such as walls and windows. Notice the different shapes and discuss the colours and textures. Ask the children about their own homes. Encourage them to tell you their house names, numbers and street names.

Give each child a zigzag book and help them to find the front page. Then invite them to talk about and decide how they are going to decorate each page. Encourage them to use the pages in different ways, such as drawing, making a collage and writing or mark-making. Ideas could include drawing the front door of their house and adding the number on it, cutting and sticking items that are in each room, drawing or listing everyone that lives at home, and so on.

Support and extension
Invite younger children to simply stick shapes and other collage materials to different parts of the house. Challenge older children to create the story of their day at home using words, pictures and captions.

Home partnership
Encourage the children to share their zigzag books with their families in the setting. Provide finger-paints and invite parents and carers to decorate the back of the book with their handprints and their children's handprints. Copy the rhyme 'House doors' on the photocopiable sheet on page 83 for parents and carers to share with their children at home.

Further ideas
♦ Make labels and captions for different areas of the home corner, such as the bedroom and kitchen.
♦ In the home corner, place a list of telephone numbers next to the telephone, together with a notebook and pencils for messages. Put recipe cards with words and pictures next to the cooker, along with a pictorial cookbook.

Theme links
Buildings
My family
Numbers

Foundation Themes
Homes

Homes treasure basket

Group size
Up to eight children.

What you need
A basket of 20 objects found commonly in the bathroom, kitchen, bedroom and living room, with a variety of initial letter sounds; large sheet of paper; marker pen; four hoops; four large labels.

Preparation
Label the hoops with the words for, and a simple line drawing of, the bedroom, bathroom, kitchen and living room.

What to do
Ask the children to sit in a circle on the floor, and place the hoops and the basket in the centre. Invite the children to take it in turns to choose an object from the basket. Encourage them to name the object and to listen to and say the initial letter sound. Write the initial letter on the large sheet of paper for all the children to see and, as a group, think of other objects at home that begin with the same initial letter sound.

Decide which room the object is likely to be used in. Discuss the colour, shape, size and weight of the object as well as its use. Talk about where the object might be kept and highlight any safety issues.

Finally, invite the child to place the item in the relevant hoop and ask the next child to choose an item. Continue the game until all the children have had a turn.

Support and extension
With younger children, place five objects that are found in homes, that all start with the same initial letter sound, into the treasure basket. Take each object out in turn, name it, identify its initial letter sound and talk about what it is used for at home. Encourage older children to listen for and identify final letter sounds.

Home partnership
Ask parents and carers to help their children to choose and bring in an object from home that begins with the same letter sound as their own name.

Further ideas
♦ Provide examples of initial letter shapes for the children to cut out. Help them to add texture to their letters with a variety of collage materials and to make a treasure basket of objects from the setting that begin with that letter sound.
♦ Choose an initial letter sound and, with a small group of children, take it in turns to name objects beginning with that letter sound from particular areas of a home. For example, an item from the kitchen that begins with the letter 'c' could be a cup or a colander.

Theme links
All about me
Letters and sounds

On the stairs

Early Learning Goal
Recognise numerals 1 to 9.

What to do

Sing the song 'When I'm going up (down) the stairs', then let each child choose a play person. Give the first child up to nine bricks from the remaining pile of bricks. Help them to count the bricks and then move their play person up that number of steps. Count the pile of bricks again and check that it matches the number on the sticky label. Continue the game for all the children.

Next, ask each child to move their play person up or down the steps. For example, say, 'Can you move your person up three steps?'. Count to three together and look at the number on the step. Continue playing until each child has had a turn at moving their play person up or down the steps.

Support and extension

With younger children, sing 'The Grand Old Duke of York' (Traditional) as they move their play people up and down the steps. Introduce a dice for older children and encourage each child to move their play person up or down the number of steps that matches their throw on the dice.

Home partnership

Ask parents and carers to help their children to count how many steps they have at home. Send home an outline of a house for them to complete together, adding the number of their house on the front door, the number of windows and the number of stairs.

Further ideas

♦ Using sticky labels, number soft balls or beanbags from 1 to 9. Have two plastic, different-coloured boxes and ask the children to take it in turns to throw, for example, ball number 3 into the red box, or ball number 5 into the blue box, and so on.

♦ Number nine bricks from 1 to 9 using sticky labels. Ask the children to choose a labelled brick and then build a tower of that number of bricks using the non-numbered ones.

**Theme links
Buildings
Numbers**

Foundation
Themes
Homes

House shapes

Group size
Four children.

What you need
Books and pictures featuring a variety of houses; large, square cardboard box; six sheets of plain paper; glue; marker pen.

Preparation
Glue a plain sheet of paper to each face of the cardboard box, to make a very large dice. Draw a circle, rectangle, triangle, square, semicircle and diamond on the faces of the dice.

What to do
Let the children take it in turns to throw the 'dice' and name the shape shown. Encourage them to match it to shapes that they can see in the setting, such as a rectangle matching the art paper, and then to shapes in the outside of the building, such as the rectangle matching the letter box or a brick on the wall.

Once all the children have had a turn, play the game again, but this time ask each child to match the shape to a shape that is found in the selection of house pictures and books. Look for details in the pictures and draw the children's attention to similarities in buildings that you can see around you.

Support and extension
Gather three round objects and three rectangular objects. Help younger children to sort and name the shapes, then go on a circle or rectangle hunt together around the setting. Help older children to count the number of corners and sides on the shapes that they find.

Home partnership
Make a poster for the parents' noticeboard, asking them to look for shapes in buildings as they travel about the neighbourhood with their children. Include a list of the actual shapes and some local examples, for example, triangles on the school's roof, rectangles in a shop window and diamonds in the windowpane of Number 6 School Lane.

Further ideas
♦ Take the children on a shapes treasure hunt, helping them to find a number of different shapes, for example, one triangle, two rectangles, three circles, four squares and so on.
♦ Take photographs of different shapes on local buildings and display them next to real examples of that shape, such as a photograph of a church spire along with a cone shape. Give the children gummed shapes to make pictures of their homes.
♦ Encourage the children to use sticky shapes to make pictures of houses, flats, shops, schools, churches and temples.

Theme links
Buildings
Shapes

Get connected

Early Learning Goal
Find out about and identify the uses of everyday technology

Group size
Up to six children.

What you need
White A4 paper; pens; coloured pencils; camera; access to a fax machine, alternatively an envelope, weighing scales and stamps.

Preparation
Contact another early years setting, either locally (preferably in a different environment) or from abroad. Enlist the help of the children's families and local contacts, if necessary. Ask the other setting to send you a photograph of the children in their group.

What to do
Show the children the photograph of the other children. Explain where they live and that you are going to find out more about them and their homes, and that they would like to know about the children's homes, too. Tell the children that you cannot visit them and so you will send pictures and drawings by fax.

Show the children the fax machine. Place a header sheet in it and demonstrate how to dial the number. If possible, arrange to receive a fax so that the children can see how the machine works.

Ask the children to draw pictures of their homes, then add captions, as appropriate. Write out the fax number on a large sheet of paper. At a pre-arranged time, let the children dial the number and press the 'start' button to send their pictures. Wait by the machine to receive your fax from the other setting if this has been arranged.

If you do not have access to a fax machine, visit a local shop that has one, or send your pictures by post. Ensure that the children have the opportunity to weigh the envelope at the post office.

Support and extension
Give younger children a house-shaped sheet of paper to colour and then fax or send it to the other group. Encourage older children to each fill in a header sheet, writing their name and copying the name of where the fax is being sent.

Home partnership
Invite parents and carers to send faxes at pre-arranged times or to provide contacts that may become partners in the activity. Ask them for old fax machines, keyboards or computers to use for imaginative play.

Further ideas
♦ Show the children a selection of everyday objects that use ICT at home. Talk about the equipment and how we use it in our everyday lives.
♦ Make a pretend fax machine by fixing a toy telephone to a shoebox, with slots for the fax paper to go into and out of.

Theme links
Our world
People who help us

Foundation Themes
Homes

This house is huge!

Group size
Four children.

What you need
Very large cardboard boxes; small cardboard boxes; plastic pipes; short lengths of plastic guttering; large pieces of bubble wrap and corrugated card; string; scissors; parcel tape; cardboard tubes; sheets of fabric; old rolls of wallpaper; camera.

Preparation
Clear a large space for the construction, preferably close to a wall that can be used to support the building.

What to do

Look at the different materials with the children and gather their ideas about how they could be used to build a house. Ask the children what all houses have – walls, windows, doors and a roof. Help the children to decide together how they will make each of these. Talk about how some of them could be fitted together. Allow the children to work as independently as possible, letting them take the lead and encouraging them to plan parts of it together. If necessary, help them with tying the string and managing the parcel tape. Make comments and ask open questions that will help the children to plan and complete their building work. Encourage them to talk about and suggest solutions to difficulties that they encounter.

Record the building process and completed works with photographs.

Support and extension

Simplify the materials provided and offer more help and direction for younger children. Show older children how to use the materials to make more complex joints.

Home partnership

Encourage parents and carers to visit the house with their children. Invite them to provide materials to help in the construction. If a parent is in the building trade, encourage them to visit your setting in work clothes and to explain what they do.

Further ideas

♦ Visit a DIY store to look at building materials. Feel the weight and texture of some materials and talk about how they are used in our homes.
♦ Build homes with tiny recyclable materials on a very small scale.
♦ Look at building plans and architects' drawings with older children, tracing around the walls, colouring gardens green, and so on.

Theme links
Buildings
People who help us
Shapes

Build a wall

Stepping Stone
Adjust speed or change direction to avoid obstacles.

Early Learning Goal
Move with confidence, imagination and in safety.

Group size
Four, six or eight children.

What you need
A variety of shoeboxes; brown paper; sticky tape; scissors; wheelbarrows or trolleys; traffic cones.

Preparation
Cover the shoeboxes with brown paper to resemble bricks. Arrange the traffic cones into two lines, so that the children can steer their wheelbarrows or trolleys around them.

What to do
Divide the children into two equal teams. Give each team a wheelbarrow or trolley and half of the 'bricks'. Explain to the children that they are going to use the bricks to build a wall at the end of the 'road', but that the road has lots of traffic cones that they need to steer around.

Invite the first child from each team to set off with a single brick in their wheelbarrow or trolley. Encourage each child to steer around the cones, place the first brick down for their wall at the other end of the 'road' and return the wheelbarrow to the next child in their line. The children should then continue to take it in turns to load a brick into the wheelbarrow, negotiate the cones and add the brick to the wall. If the wall falls down, the children must take all the bricks back to the start and begin again.

Continue playing until both teams have finished their walls.

Support and extension
Encourage younger children to fill the wheelbarrow or trolley with bricks and then tip them down next to the wall. Let older children negotiate pushing the wheelbarrow or trolley through tunnels, along planks and over bumps made from corrugated card.

Home partnership
Invite parents and carers to come to collect their children a few minutes earlier at the end of the session to try this activity with them. Add an 'outdoor-play ideas' section to the parents' noticeboard, adding a new idea each week.

Further ideas
♦ Set up an obstacle course for the children to get around. Finish with a large box that is 'Teddy's home'. Ask the children to take a teddy or other soft toy around the obstacle course and get it home safely.
♦ Use trolleys, wheelbarrows and bikes outdoors to role-play moving house.
♦ Sing the song 'My wheelbarrow' on the photocopiable sheet on page 86.

Theme links
Buildings
Wheels

Foundation
Themes
Homes

Threading fun

Group size
Up to six children.

What you need
Six sheets of thin card; marker pen; coloured pencils; scissors; sticky tape; single hole-punch; ribbon; string; cord; electric-cable casing; bendy straws; raffia; wool.

Preparation
Draw and cut out a home shape on each piece of card. Make each card a different style of house, for example, flats, terraces, detached, cottages and so on.

What to do

Ask each child to select a card and encourage them to talk about the building that they have chosen and why. Help them to use the single hole-punch to make several holes for threading around the edge of their card. Let them colour their house shape and then invite them to use a variety of the threading materials to carefully weave in and out of the holes.

Secure the end of each threading length with sticky tape on the back of the card, then encourage each child to add their name to their work.

Support and extension

Prepare the card with holes for younger children and help them to thread with the thickest cord. Wrap sticky tape around the threading end tightly to make it easier for the cord to go through the holes. Encourage older children to fix several homes together to make a street. Add a range of collage materials for them to complete their scene.

Home partnership

Ask parents and carers to provide materials for this activity. Send home a second card, already prepared with the holes, for the children to complete with their families.

Further ideas

♦ Let the children make houses from play dough and encourage them to create features using lolly sticks and pasta shapes. Place each house on a square of paper, then arrange all the homes together to make a street scene.
♦ Use a range of safe building materials for printing, such as plastic pipes, brick facings, wood, polystyrene tiles and so on.
♦ Make a 'homes mobile'. Ask each child to cut out a house shape and decorate it with paint and collage materials. Attach all the shapes together to create a mobile and hang it from your ceiling.

Theme links
Buildings
Colours

Foundation
Themes
Homes

My front door

Stepping Stone
Choose particular colours to use for a purpose.

Early Learning Goal
Explore colour, texture, shape, form and space in two or three dimensions.

Group size
Four children.

What you need
Cereal box for each child; pencils; marker pen; scissors; collage materials; glue; sticky tape; paint; paintbrushes; plastic bricks; plain paper; the rhyme 'House doors' on the photocopiable sheet on page 83.

Preparation
Turn the cereal boxes inside out and stick them together. Make sure that you know the street name and number or name of house for each child's home.

What to do
Read the rhyme 'House doors' on the photocopiable sheet. Talk to the children about their front doors and what they can see when they open them. Discuss colours and textures, house numbers, letter boxes and door furniture.

Give each child a cereal box and help them to draw and cut out a front door, leaving it as a flap that can open and close. Comment on each child's work as they use paint and collage materials to decorate the front of their home and their front door, encouraging them to think about their own home. Invite the children to use the plastic bricks to create a brick effect on the walls of their homes.

Next, help each child to draw a picture of themselves, or of members of their family, to glue inside the box, so that when they open their front door, they can see themselves or their family.

Support and extension
Provide younger children with plain paper and encourage them to print or sponge-paint their front doors. Use the marker pen to add their house or flat number or name. Let older children paint or print some paper to line their boxes to make them look like their hallways.

Home partnership
Provide the children with wax crayons and ask parents and carers to help them to do a wax-rubbing picture of the different shapes and textures on the front of their house, such as the bricks, the lines between floor tiles or the patterns on the glass.

Further ideas
♦ Play the game 'My street' on the photocopiable sheet on page 91 to practise number recognition and counting.
♦ Photocopy a street map of your area and highlight the shops, park and library. Show the children the main roads and bus stops and help each child to identify where they live. Encourage them to write their name on a sticky star and to place it appropriately on the map.

Theme links
All about me
My family
My neighbourhood

Foundation Themes
Homes

Rhythm and rhyme

Group size
Four to six children.

What you need
A beater or small wooden spoon for each child; piece of wood, plastic guttering, pipe or tile for each child (at least one of each).

Preparation
Ensure that you are familiar with the rhymes, 'My Little House Won't Stand Up Straight' and 'Build a House with Five Bricks' both from This Little Puffin... compiled by Elizabeth Matterson (Puffin Books).

What to do

Sing the rhymes with the children, then tap out the rhythm of the first line of the first rhyme as you sing the tune again. Give each child a beater and piece of wood, plastic, pipe or tile. Listen to the sounds that each one makes. Tap out the first line of rhyme together and continue to sing or say the remainder of the rhyme. Repeat this for the second rhyme.

Now, encourage the children to listen very carefully as you tap out the first line of one of the rhymes without any singing. Can the children name the rhyme? Tap it out again, this time invite the children to sing and tap out the rhythm together. Continue to tap out the first lines of the rhymes, encouraging the children to listen and name the tune each time.

Support and extension

With younger children, sit opposite two children and sing the action rhyme 'Build a House with Five Bricks', encouraging them to copy your actions. Invite older children to tap out one of the rhymes for the rest of the group to name.

Home partnership

Ask parents and carers to help their children to choose an object from home to bring in for your rhythm band, such as an old pan, a box of rice as a shaker and so on. Send home a copy of one of the rhymes that you have been singing for the children to share with their families.

Further ideas

♦ Adapt the traditional rhyme 'The Wheels on the Bus' to sounds found at home, such as 'The bell in the porch goes "ding-a-ling-a-ling"' or 'The timer on the cooker goes "buzz buzz buzz"' and so on.
♦ Go on a sounds walk with the children around your setting and explore how the different materials of the building, such as metal, plastic or brick. sound when they are tapped. Ask the children what sounds they can make at home.

Theme links
Buildings
Materials
Music

Chapter 2

Inside my home

In the early years, children's learning and interests develop from the security and familiarity of home. This chapter focuses on familiar routines at home, people who visit homes and what we have in our homes, including everyday technology.

Group size
Whole group, working in groups of up to three children.

What you need
An example of patchwork, such as a cushion or quilt; sticky tape; pens; paint; collage materials; large sheet of colourful backing paper; small different-coloured paper squares, approximately 15 x 15cm, one for each child and member of staff, and one for each of the significant people in the community such as milk deliverer, postperson, crossing-patrol person, older brothers and sisters and so on.

Preparation
Encourage parents and carers to help their children with ideas of what to draw about their homes.

Theme links
Colours
My family
Patterns

Patchwork homes

What to do
Show the children the patchwork quilt or cushion and explain that you are all going to make a patchwork of pictures about homes. Talk to the children about their homes, encouraging them to tell you what makes them special, who lives there, their favourite things about their homes and their favourite songs, rhymes and story-books about homes.

Ask each child to choose one thing to draw about their home, and add a caption for them. Encourage the children to use a range of pens, paint and collage materials. Invite significant local people, such as people who deliver to the setting, or regular visitors, and older brothers and sisters, to make additional squares to add to the patchwork.

Fix the patchwork together using sticky tape on the back of the squares and place them on the backing paper, then arrange a day to celebrate the completion of the patchwork and to recognise everyone's contribution.

Stepping Stone
Show a strong sense of self as a member of different communities, such as their family or setting.

Early Learning Goal
Understand that people have different needs, views, cultures and beliefs, that need to be treated with respect.

Support and extension
Prompt younger children to talk about their homes and their favourite part, or the most important thing about them. Write their words on each child's square, then help them to add a handprint to it. Let older children make patchwork invitations and posters about the celebration.

Home partnership
Invite parents and carers to add their own squares to the patchwork quilt. Encourage them to become involved in helping to plan the celebration and ask them for their assistance on the day.

Further ideas
♦ Ask the children to bring unusual objects from their homes, such as items from other countries or from the past, for a 'From my home' show-and-tell session.
♦ Make collections of objects from home that all have a different purpose but are the same colour or texture. For example, a group of shiny objects would include metal teaspoons, kitchen foil, a mirror, baby's toys and so on.

Rainbow colours

Group size
Up to eight children.

What you need
A basket of different-coloured ribbons; copy of the song *I Can Sing a Rainbow* by Arthur Hamilton (Nellie Edge Resources).

Preparation
Familiarise yourself with the song *I Can Sing a Rainbow*.

What to do

Explain to the children that you are going to think about colours, particularly colours in their homes. Invite them to tell you, in turn, their favourite colour, the colour of their front door and also the colours in their bedroom. Sing together the song *I Can Sing a Rainbow*.

Next, pass the basket of coloured ribbons around the group and ask each child to choose a ribbon that is the same colour as an object in their home, such as a blanket, a cushion or a rug. Encourage them to tell the group what colour they have chosen and which object it matches from home. Ask them to explain or comment on their choice. After each child has spoken, place the ribbon on the floor to make a rainbow with the other ribbons.

Finish by singing the song *I Can Sing a Rainbow*. Leave the ribbons out for the children to explore further.

Support and extension

Ask younger children to each tell you the colour of their blanket at home and then to find a ribbon of the same colour. Encourage older children to find colours that match objects at home from a specific room, or for a specific purpose, saying, for example, 'Choose a ribbon that matches something from your home that is used for washing up'.

Home partnership

Let each child choose a ribbon to take home and ask parents and carers to help their children to select an object of the same colour to bring into the setting.

Further ideas

♦ Gather together objects of different textures and materials, such as smooth wood, fur, wool, stretchy fabric, glass and so on. Talk with the children about objects inside homes that are of similar textures and made from similar materials.

♦ Ask the children what they think the most precious object is in their homes. Talk about 'treasure' from your own home, such as a favourite photograph, a teddy bear from your childhood and so on.

Theme links
Colours
Materials

Foundation
Themes
Homes

My day

Group size
Four to six children.

What you need
The photocopiable sheet 'My routine' on page 92; thin card; cord or ribbon to make a washing line; pegs; box of items to represent the sequence of the day, such as a cup and bowl for breakfast, clothes for getting dressed, coat and keys for going out, apron for painting in the setting, story-book for story time, ball for playing outside, plate for teatime, and pyjamas and blanket for bedtime; pen.

Preparation
Fix a washing line well within the reach of the smallest child. Copy the photocopiable sheet on to thin card and cut out the pictures.

What to do
Talk to the children about their routines at home. Ask them what they do first when they wake up. As each part of a day is described, lay out the objects on the floor or table to show the sequence of the routine throughout the day.

Look at the pictures and tell the children about your usual routine, then help them to lay the pictures in the order of your day.

Next, arrange four of the items or pictures and ask the children to tell you what is happening first. Go through each part of the routine and ask open-ended questions to encourage the children to comment on their own routines.

Help the children to peg the pictures on the washing line in the order of their day and talk about how the routines may be different for families in different homes.

Support and extension
With younger children, talk about one part of their day, for example, bedtime. Ask them to find objects and pictures that represent bedtime, such as the pyjamas and the picture of the bed and teddy. With older children, talk about morning, afternoon, daytime and night. Help them to think about the family routine and how it fits with their day, such as when their baby sister wakes up.

Home partnership
Ask parents and carers to talk to their children about their own routines when they were children.

Further ideas
♦ Talk about shift work and how some people sleep at home during the day, because they have been at work all night.
♦ Ask the children to peg three items from home that all have the same purpose on the washing line, such as three items used to make dinner.

Theme links
All about me
My family

Foundation Themes
Homes

Letters and parcels

Stepping Stone
Initiate conversation, attend to and take account of what others say, and use talk to resolve disagreements.

Group size
Four to six children.

What you need
A large sheet of card; large box; red paper; postcards; envelopes; pens; scissors; sticky labels; post bag; wrapping paper; shoeboxes; string; telephone directory; packaging and envelopes from items recently posted to your home.

Preparation
Set up letter-writing and parcel-making activities, with pretend stamps, in the home corner. Use the large sheet of card to make a front door with a letter box for the home corner. Place some of the postcards in envelopes. Cover the large box with red paper to make a post-box, by sealing it with sticky tape and cutting a slit in the front. Leave a flap for emptying the box.

What to do

Tell the children how excited you feel when you hear the post arriving at your home. Ask why the postperson might ring the bell instead of using the letter box.

Early Learning Goal
Interact with others, negotiating plans and activities.

Talk about the sort of post that may arrive in people's homes, such as brown or white envelopes, postcards, leaflets, magazines and parcels. Look at the envelopes and packaging of the post that you have received and invite the children to guess what might have been inside. Examine the stamps and addresses. Can the children find the house number?

Place all the envelopes and parcels in the pretend post-box and invite a child to empty the box and deliver them to the role-play house.

Give the children plenty of time to open envelopes and parcels, write cards and wrap parcels and to post them in the post-box. Include cards and envelopes with the children's names on the front. Help the children to share out the post.

Support and extension

Encourage younger children to empty and fill the post-box with cards, carefully posting the items, one at a time. Invite older children to deliver cards around the setting, looking at the initial letters to help them to guess who each item is for.

Home partnership

Encourage parents and carers to look at the addresses on their post with their children. Suggest that they let their children open some of the envelopes and sort the post together. Ask them to bring in old envelopes and packaging for the parcel-making table.

Further ideas

♦ Invite the local postperson to visit your setting to show the children their uniform, bags and bicycle or van.
♦ Sing the song 'The postie's bag' on the photocopiable sheet on page 87.

Theme links
Numbers
People who help us

Numbers everywhere!

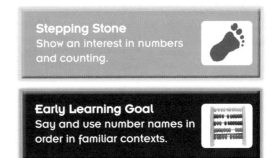

Early Learning Goal
Say and use number names in order in familiar contexts.

Group size
Up to eight children.

What you need
Items that have numbers on them and are commonly found in homes, such as a television remote control, telephone directory, weighing scales, recipe book, calculator, clock, telephone, coins and calendar; sticky labels; pens; wide range of recyclable, collage and paint materials; low bench; paper.

Preparation
Clear some wall space to create a linear display of pictures and models and place some of the home items on a low bench.

What to do
Show the children some of the home items and talk about their uses. Think about each room in the home and ask what other objects have numbers. For example, in the bathroom, numbers may appear on the bathroom scales and on the side of the shampoo bottle.

Ask the children to choose one of the objects and create a model or picture of that object. Help them to use the labels to add numbers to their work. Display the paintings and models on the low bench, next to some of the home items. Add a large number line to the display so that the children can match the numbers on their work to those on the number line.

Support and extension
Allow plenty of time for younger children to handle the objects. With three-year-olds, look for and find the number 3 on each item, and so on, according to the age of each child. Encourage older children to find a specific number on each object, for example, number 6.

Home partnership
Ask parents and carers to help their children to find an object with numbers on in their homes to add to the collection. Send home a song sheet with some favourite number rhymes, together with the rhyme 'Click, click, click' on the photocopiable sheet on page 84.

Further ideas
♦ Look at a range of clocks and pictures of clocks from homes, such as kitchen clocks, timers, grandfather clocks and digital clocks. Look at the way that the numerals are arranged and sing the traditional rhyme 'Hickory Dickory Dock'.
♦ Label five bricks numbered 1 to 5 and sing the traditional rhyme 'Build a House with Five Bricks'.

Theme links
Machines
Numbers
Time

Foundation Themes
Homes

Home patterns

Group size
Four children.

What you need
Large sheets of plain paper; sticky tape; scissors; paint in small trays; range of washable household objects found in a bathroom, such as a nailbrush, sponge, toothbrush, and bath toy; items found in a kitchen such as cup, fork, fish slice and washing-up brush; items found in a living room such as a leaf from a house plant and a coaster; items found in a bedroom such as a plastic comb and a plastic bangle.

Preparation
Cut the paper into long strips, approximately 10cm wide, and fix them together to make four long banners or borders.

What to do
Explain to the children that you are going to make some wallpaper for the home corner. Sort all the objects into separate piles, each pile corresponding to the part of a home where they are used. Talk about the colour, shape and texture of each object and encourage the children to think about the patterns that it will make when it is used to print on paper.

Let each child choose a group of objects from one room of a home and help them to make a repeating pattern on the paper after dipping the objects in the trays of paint. For example, if they have chosen the bathroom, they could use a sponge, toothbrush and bath toy to print with. Encourage the children to look at the shapes that the objects make and to try out different patterns, asking open questions to help them to see and comment on the patterns.

When the banners are dry, use them to decorate the home corner and define each of the rooms, such as the kitchen, bedroom and so on.

Support and extension
Encourage younger children to talk about the objects as they print randomly on paper. Let older children create more complex patterns by adding pictures, such as food items, cut from magazines and brochures, on to their kitchen banner.

Home partnership
Send home a blank banner for each child to decorate. Suggest a pattern, such as a clock, shoe, teddy, clock and so on. The children could draw or cut pictures from magazines to complete their banners.

Further ideas
♦ Choose some larger objects found in a home, such as a toy-box and waste-paper basket. Help the children to use chalk to draw around these objects outside. Look at the different chalk outlines and match them to the real objects.
♦ Make some simple card templates of household items such as a cup, spoon, key and so on. Help the children to draw around the templates on black and white paper and to cut them out. Use the shapes to make some shadow pictures.

Theme links
All about me
Shapes

Can you guess?

Stepping Stone
Examine objects to find out more about them.

Early Learning Goal
Investigate objects and materials by using all of their senses as appropriate.

Group size
Up to six children.

What you need
Pillowcase or similar soft bag; weighing scales; tape measure; stacking bricks; string; scissors; large sheet of paper; pen; selection of objects found in homes, of varying size, weight, colour, material and function, such as a metal spoon, plastic bowl, bathroom sponge, heavy book and remote control.

Preparation
Place one of the objects in the pillowcase and keep the rest of the objects well hidden.

What to do
Give the pillowcase to a child and invite them to feel and peek inside.
Say that they must not show or tell the other children what the object is. Explain that the object is something that is found in homes and invite the children to take turns to ask about questions about it. They may ask about its colour, shape, size and function, which room it is used in or what material it is made of. Prompt a range of questions that will help the children to think about the object and its use.

When each child has asked a question, invite them to guess what the object is. Reveal the object and pass it around, then help the children to measure it using different methods, for example, cut a piece of string the same length as the object, stack bricks to the same height or length as the object, count how many bricks you need to match the weight of the object and so on. Help the children to record the information using pictures, numbers and symbols on the large sheet of paper.

Repeat the game using the other home items.

Support and extension
With younger children, place an object in the pillowcase, and let them feel it and guess what the object is before passing the pillowcase to the next child. Provide simple clues, describing the object by its use. For older children, place two related objects in the pillowcase, such as a toothbrush and toothpaste.

Home partnership
Ask parents and carers to play 'Kim's Game' with home objects, placing up to six objects on a tray, covering the tray, removing one object and then taking turns with their child to guess which object has been removed.

Further ideas
♦ Try out the recipe on the photocopiable sheet 'Gingerbread houses' on page 93.
♦ Extend the home-corner equipment to reflect a wider range of cultures, for example, adding chopsticks in the kitchen.

Theme links
Materials
Measuring

Foundation Themes
Homes

In the kitchen

Group size
Four children.

What you need
Dried pasta and cooked pasta; packet of jelly and a made-up jelly; flour; cup; plastic bottle; water droppers; whisk; wooden spoon; metal spoons; slotted spoons; mashers; rolling-pin; sieves; funnels; plastic bowls; plates; children's knives and forks; aprons; kitchen scales; plastic measuring jug.

Preparation
Cover all surfaces. This is a very messy activity that may be best carried out outdoors!

What to do
Look at the different items of kitchen equipment with the children and talk about what they are used for and what they are made of. Discuss their colour, shape and texture.

Next, look at the measuring jug and weighing scales, then weigh some items together. Talk about the differences between the cooked and dried pasta, and between the packet of jelly and the made-up jelly.

Allow plenty of time for the children to explore the materials, by mixing, chopping and mashing, using all the utensils available.

Sit alongside the children, commenting on what they are doing and what you can see. Look for any changes in colour and texture.

Next, invite each child to count out five spoonfuls of flour and measure a cupful of water, then let them play freely with the mixture. Make a simple flour-and-water mix and talk about the way that the dough forms. Knead the dough, roll it out and share it with the children, then encourage them to make their own dough mixtures. Give the time to play and test out their ideas.

Support and extension
Make a simple cornflour-and-water mix for younger children and give them wooden spoons to mix and drop the mixture. Encourage them to use their hands to explore the mixture. With older children, talk about solids and liquids and how the ingredients change as they play.

Home partnership
Send home a play-dough recipe and a list of everyday home objects that the children can use in the dough.

Further ideas
♦ Make up some bread dough with the children, watching the ingredients change as they are mixed and kneaded, and then baked.
♦ Add a variety of ingredients to water, one at a time, and talk about what is happening. Try mxing sugar, adding food-colouring drops or sprinkling flour on to the surface.
♦ Sing the song 'Kitchen song' on the photocopiable sheet on page 87.

Theme links
Changes
Food

Sleeping, eating, having fun!

Group size
Whole group.

What you need
Four very large banners, labelled with words such as 'kitchen', 'living room', 'bedroom', 'bathroom', 'garden' and so on, decorated with pictures representing these areas.

Preparation
Hang the banners in four different areas or corners of the setting.

What to do
Talk to the children about the sorts of exercise that they take, such as playing outside, riding bikes, going to the park, playing football, swimming, dancing, walking and so on. Discuss the way that our bodies change when we exercise, for example, getting warm, sweating and breathing hard, and also the way that they change after we have exercised regularly, such as getting stronger and quicker and helping us to be healthy.

Tell the children that a lot of what we do at home is about getting and keeping healthy and well. For example, when we eat, we help our bodies to grow, and we sleep in order to have energy.

Show the children the banners. Explain that when you call out an activity, you would like them to think about the room or area in which they do the activity at home and then go to the corresponding banner. Call out different activities and routines that the children carry out at home, for example, eating breakfast, washing teeth, having a rest, sleeping, playing football and so on, and help the children to move to the appropriate banner. After each activity, ask the children how the action keeps us healthy.

Support and extension
Play with up to four younger children and place relevant objects under each banner, such as a teddy and blanket under the bedroom banner, to help them understand the game. Give older children a chance to be the caller, using their own ideas for healthy activities.

Home partnership
Put details of local parks, swimming-pool sessions and play areas on the parents' noticeboard. Encourage parents and carers to post 'for sale' notices for bikes and outdoor toys on the board.

Further ideas
◆ Invite the children's older brothers and sisters to visit your setting in their sports kit and to ask them to tell the children about their exercise and play activities.
◆ Ask parents and carers for old rackets and organise a tennis or badminton play time for the children.

Theme links
Outdoor play
Keeping healthy

We all put on shoes

Stepping Stone
Respond to rhythm, music and story by means of gesture and movement.

Early Learning Goal
Move with confidence, imagination and in safety.

Group size
Up to eight children.

What you need
Cup; bowl and spoon; hat; trousers; shoes; coat; flannel; toothbrush; hairbrush; story-book; bricks; teddy blanket.

Preparation
Make sure that you are familiar with the traditional song 'We All Clap Hands Together' from *This Little Puffin...* compiled by Elizabeth Matterson (Puffin Books).

What to do
Ask the children to sit in a circle and place all the objects on the floor in the centre. Go through the objects and talk about the routines at home, such as getting up, eating breakfast, getting dressed and so on. Ask the children to stand and hold hands ready for the game. Start by singing the chorus 'We all clap hands together'.

Next, invite a child to choose an object from the centre, such as the shoes, and mime the action, then all sing together:

We all put on shoes together,
We all put on shoes together,
We all put on shoes together,
As children like to do.

Sing the chorus of the traditional song again, and then ask the next child to choose an object. Continue the game, singing, dancing and choosing items, until they have all have been used.

Support and extension
Play with three younger children, and a second adult to help, if necessary. Encourage older children to choose objects in order, for example, what they would use first thing in the morning, followed by when they are getting washed and dressed, then when they play, with the bedtime objects last.

Home partnership
Encourage parents and carers to borrow songbooks and nursery rhymes cassette tapes or traditional songs cassette tapes. Invest in a high-quality nursery rhymes audio or video tape and make it available for loan to families.

Further ideas
♦ Sing the song 'I wake up at seven o'clock' on the photocopiable sheet on page 88 with the children.
♦ Make the objects available for free play in the home corner, encouraging the children to act out the routines that you talked about.

Theme links
Clothes
Routines

Foundation Themes
Homes

The bears' house

Group size
Four children.

What you need
A copy of the story 'Goldilocks and the Three Bears' (Traditional); large, medium and small chair, blanket, spoon and bowl; dressing-up clothes corresponding to the story's characters, in a large box or suitcase; porridge oats; milk; play food; the song 'When Goldilocks Went to the House of the Bears' from the CD *Children's Favourites* (Early Learning Centre); CD player.

Preparation
Make some porridge, allow it to cool and share it between the three bowls. Familiarise yourself with the story of Goldilocks and with the song.

What to do
Read the story 'Goldilocks and the Three Bears' to the children, then look back through the story-book at the pictures, recapping the main parts of the story. Let each child choose their role within the story: Daddy Bear, Mummy Bear, Baby Bear and Goldilocks. Help them to select their dressing-up clothes, arrange their blankets and chairs, and set the table with their bowls of porridge. Slowly retell the story and encourage the children to act out the tale with the props. Give them plenty of time and allow them to add their own ideas. At the end, sing the song 'When Goldilocks Went to the House of the Bears'.

Next, let the children swap roles and repeat the story. Let the story and play develop along the children's own ideas, following their lead and asking open questions to help them to develop their own thinking about the story.

Check for any food allergies or dietary requirements.

Support and extension
Sing the song with younger children, allowing them to explore the props. Encourage older children to imagine what might have happened next, where Goldilocks has gone, what the bears do next, and so on.

Home partnership
Send home an outline of the tale for parents and carers to share with their children.

Further ideas
♦ Read *Alfie Gets in First* by Shirley Hughes (Red Fox) to the children and help them to role-play this story in the home corner, providing a front-door key and a pushchair for Annie Rose, as props.
♦ Ask the children to tell you about any experiences that they have had of moving house, then create a simple imaginary tale about moving house.

Theme links
All about me
Families
Food

My treasure bag

Stepping Stone
Understand that different media can be combined.

Early Learning Goal
Explore colour, texture, shape, form and space in two or three dimensions.

Group size
Two or three children.

What you need
A small piece of thick card; scissors; marker pen; coloured pens; small pieces of paper; glue; strong glue; buttons; sequins; sticky paper shapes; Cellophane; foil; glitter; lengths of ribbon; selection of plain and patterned fabric pieces, of different colours and textures.

Preparation
Cut a house-shaped template from the thick card.

What to do

Help each child to choose some fabric to make a house-shaped treasure bag, by drawing twice around the template on to the fabric and then cutting out the house shapes.

Invite each child to decorate their bag with the collage materials and glitter. Talk about the different patterns and shapes that can be made with the materials. Encourage each child to feel all the materials and choose carefully which ones they want to use.

Next, fix the front and back of the bag together with strong glue, leaving the roof area as the opening of the bag. Add ribbons for handles. Then encourage each child to draw a picture of their home on a piece of paper, or write or make marks about their favourite thing at home.

When the treasure bags are complete, show them for everyone to see, and talk about each child's picture or writing.

Support and extension

With younger children, prepare fabric bags and help them to choose and explore collage materials to decorate their bags. Let older children sew large buttons on to their bags and cut a felt or fabric fringe for further decoration.

Home partnership

Encourage the children to bring in their favourite small toys from home to add to their treasure bags for a show-and-tell session. Invite parents and carers to help their children to select photos of themselves or their families to add to their treasure bags.

Further ideas

♦ Include in your selection of materials things to add to water, such as sand, soap powder, flour and so on, to create different effects.
♦ Add dried pasta shapes, cotton reels, buttons and lolly sticks to play dough to make models of houses. Use Cellophane and thick card for windows and roof tiles.

Theme links
Colours
Patterns
Senses

Foundation Themes
Homes

Chapter 3

My home, my street

As children grow in confidence in the early years, they become increasingly interested in their surroundings and how they and their home fit into their wider community and neighbourhood. This chapter provides a range of exciting activities looking at places close to home and of special importance to children, such as the library, shops and post office.

Pizza houses

Group size
Four children.

What you need
Baking trays; clean dough cutting tools; rolling-pins; pizza-dough mix; toppings such as cheese slices, sliced ham, sliced chicken, pineapple, tomato sauce, tinned cannellini beans, green beans and broccoli, all on plates.

Preparation
Trim, wash and blanche the broccoli and green beans in boiling water for five minutes and allow to cool.

What to do
Stand at the gate of your setting with the children and look at the shapes of the buildings that you can see. Talk about the tall walls, steep roofs, shapes of windows and doors, colours and textures. Go back inside and ask the children about buildings on their street. How are they different? Do they see other buildings on the way home, such as churches and shops? Talk about the similarities and differences of these buildings.

Stepping Stone
Relate and make attachments to members of their group.

Early Learning Goal
Form good relationships with adults and peers.

Invite the children to choose one of the buildings that they saw outside and explain that they are going to make a building-shaped pizza. Follow the pizza-dough recipe on the packet, allowing the children to be as independent as possible.

Next, share the dough between the children. Help each child to roll their dough out and to use the dough tools to cut a basic building shape and add textures and patterns, such as brickwork and roof tiles. Then help them to spread the tomato sauce on to the pizza base and to cut carefully and add toppings to make windows, doors, chimneys and so on. Use spare dough to make road, car or bus shapes.

Bake the pizzas and share them with the rest of the group.

Support and extension
With younger children, focus on the dough-making process, encouraging turn-taking. Make one large pizza, taking it in turns to add toppings and talking together about the patterns that you are making. Older children can plan out their pizzas on paper before making their pizza building.

Home partnership
Send home a pizza-house outline on a sheet of paper and ask the children and their families to design together their own pizza house, drawing and colouring the toppings on to the outline.

Further ideas
♦ Make dough using a simple biscuit recipe or cookie mix and encourage the children to use cutters to make building-shaped biscuits to share at snack time.
♦ Play a circle game, encouraging each child to tell the group about their favourite food at home.

Theme links
Food
Keeping healthy
Shapes

Foundation Themes
Homes

Our homes

Stepping Stone
Persist for extended periods of time at an activity of their choosing.

Early Learning Goal
Continue to be interested, excited and motivated to learn.

Group size
Four children.

What you need
Plastic bricks; sticky labels; pens; A4 coloured paper; glue; sticky tape; scissors; number line; ribbon; recyclable model materials; the rhyme 'Friends and neighbours' on the photocopiable sheet on page 84.

Preparation
Find out the number for each child's home.

What to do

Read the rhyme 'Friends and neighbours' on the photocopiable sheet to the children. Explain to them that they are going to make models of their own or friends' homes or front doors. Tell them that they can either build the homes with bricks or recyclable materials, or they can make front-door flaps with the coloured paper (see below).

To make a front-door flap, give each child two sheets of A4 coloured paper. Ask them to draw the front door on the first sheet of paper and help them to cut carefully along one side, and then along the top and bottom of the door. Next, glue this to the second sheet of paper and let the children draw a person on it through the opened door.

To build a house with the plastic bricks or the recyclable materials, help the children to select the bricks or the materials and to make the house. Then for each model, encourage them to draw a picture of whose home it is and place this inside the house. Invite the children to write the house number on a sticky label, using the number line for guidance.

Arrange all the models and paper front doors on a table, then ask the children to cut lengths of ribbon and stretch them from one house to another. Encourage them to fix the ribbons in place with sticky tape to link the homes, emphasising the bonds and friendships between friends and neighbours.

LEGO house
Front door
Sticky-label house number

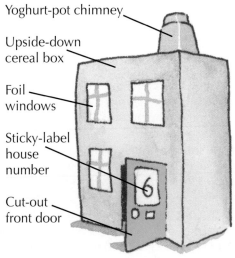

Yoghurt-pot chimney
Upside-down cereal box
Foil windows
Sticky-label house number
Cut-out front door

Sheet of paper
Front-door drawing

Support and extension

For younger children, use larger bricks to build a house or give each child a front-door shape to colour or paint the same colour as their own front door. Encourage older children to make a complex web of models, including their friends' homes.

Home partnership

Leave the materials out and invite parents and carers to make a house with their children to add to the models.

Further ideas

♦ Set up a street scene, labelling local buildings and adding a model of your setting.
♦ With the children, make a list of drawings of the main local buildings. Copy the list for each child and go for a walk in small groups around your neighbourhood, asking the children to colour in each building as they spot it.

Theme links
Buildings
Numbers
Our town

At the library

Stepping Stone
Use language for an increasing range of purposes.

Early Learning Goal
Speak clearly and audibly with confidence and control and show awareness of the listener, for example by their use of conventions such as greetings, 'please' and 'thank you'.

Group size
Four children.

What you need
The photocopiable sheet 'Tickets and bookmarks' on page 94; large box containing inkpads and stamps, Post-it notes, children's books, adults' paperback books, library tickets, dressing-up clothes, keyboard or old computer, 'Open' and 'Closed' signs, telephone, pens, notepads, doll, pushchair and noticeboard.

Preparation
Visit your local library to return and borrow some books and to look around in both the adults and children sections. Make sure that the children watch the librarian stamping tickets, entering details on the computer and so on. Copy the templates on the photocopiable sheet on to card and cut them out to make tickets and bookmarks, using the space at the top for each child's name and the blank space below for a drawing or to stick on to the child's photograph.

Theme links
Our town
People who help us

What to do
Look through the prop box with the children, discussing each item and how it is used in the library. Together, set up a role-play library area, encouraging the children to make labels for different areas, for example, 'Picture books', and using their ideas on how to arrange furniture and props.

Invite each child to choose if they are going to be the librarian, an adult selecting new books, an adult with a baby visiting the library, a child wanting to choose a different book, and so on. Role-play returning a book, modelling conventional greetings, for example, 'Good morning, I would like to return three books, please'.

Allow plenty of time for the children to play, adding new props or ideas as needed. Make comments and ask open questions to help the children to develop their ideas, such as, 'Oh dear, I think that book is already out – what can we do?'.

Support and extension
With younger children, stay more involved, taking on the role of the librarian or the visitor bringing tickets and books for stamping and returning. With older children, introduce the idea of fines for overdue books, providing coins and a purse.

Home partnership
Add directions to your local library on the parents' noticeboard, including opening times and details of children's activities and story time at the library. Encourage parents and carers to contribute appropriate props for the role-play.

Further ideas
♦ Ask people of particular relevance from your local community to visit, such as the crossing patrol person, local community police officer, health visitor and so on.
♦ Set up a rental store outside with the children, swapping tickets for the loan of bicycles or other wheeled toys.

Foundation
Themes
Homes

Out of my window

Group size
Six children.

What you need
Small pieces of card; marker pen.

Preparation
Familiarise yourself with the popular memory game 'Granny Went to Market'.

What to do

Sit together in a circle and explain that you are going to play a listening-and-remembering' game. Start with 'One day I was looking out of my window when I saw a dog'. Draw a simple dog on a piece of card and place it face down in front of you. Turn to the child next to you and prompt them by saying, 'One day I was looking out of my window when I saw a dog and a…'. Help the child to think of something that they can see out of their window at home and add this to the list, saying, 'One day I was looking out of my window when I saw a dog and a bus'. Draw a bus on a piece of card and place it face down in front of the child.

Continue going around the circle, helping each child to add another item that they can see from their window at home and using the cards as prompts. When all the children have had a turn, give yourselves a clap and begin again, but this time say, 'I went to town and visited the…', for example, 'post office', 'bakery', 'shoe shop' and so on. As before, use simple drawings as prompts, such as a letter for the post office, some apples for the fruit shop, and so on.

Support and extension

For younger children, play a game with three objects, such as a car, doll, and hat. Say 'When I looked out of my window I saw a car, a baby and a man with a hat'. Cover the objects and ask the children to recall what you saw. Encourage older children to draw their own prompt cards.

Home partnership

Explain to parents and carers how to play the game inside and how they could turn it into a travel game when waiting for the bus or queuing at the shops.

Further ideas

♦ Make a tape of sounds heard in homes, such as a clock ticking, a switched-on vacuum cleaner or someone washing-up. Ask the children to listen carefully and name the sounds.

♦ Go on a listening walk around your area. See how many sounds you can recall when you get back.

Theme links
Sounds
People who help us

Where are you going?

Stepping Stone
Describe a simple journey.

Early Learning Goal
Use everyday words to describe position.

Group size
Three to four children.

What you need
A road mat; small cars; buses; play people; train track and trains; small-world buildings; sticky labels; pens; paper; scissors.

Preparation
Set out the road mat, cars, buses and train track in a clear space. Use the sticky labels to mark the buildings as 'school', 'shops', 'library', 'swimming-pool' and so on, adding symbols, for example, a book next to the word 'library'. Use the paper to make a set of tickets, writing each of the labelled buildings as a destination on them.

What to do

Give each child a few play people and ask them to choose one of the tickets. Place the first play person on the edge of the road mat and ask the children how they could get this person to their destination. Match the destination on the ticket to the labelled building.

Ask open questions and make comments to help the children explain the journey that is required, for example, talk about town and country, ask how far the destination is and if the person will walk or go by train, bus or car.

Invite the children to talk about their own journeys to the setting, what they see, how they travel, how long it takes and so on. Encourage the use of words and phrases that describe position, such as 'close to', 'alongside', 'in front of', 'behind', 'next to' and so on.

Support and extension

Ask younger children to steer a small car around the road mat to get to specific destinations. Provide a commentary for their journeys, using simple words and phrases to describe them. Invite older children to make their own tickets and decide on their destination, for example, a ticket for two to school.

Home partnership

Make a list of all the children's names and ask parents and carers to help their children to find their names, and add a picture to describe how they get to the setting, such as by car, by bus or walking.

Further ideas

♦ Use chalks to draw a garage, car wash and shop on different floor areas outside. Help the children to make tickets and then ride their bikes to the different destinations. As each child takes their ticket, ask them to tell you about their journey, which way they will go, who they will pass and so on.
♦ Read the story *Mr Gumpy's Motor Car* by John Burningham (Red Fox) and talk about the journey and the places that the car passes through.

Theme links
Buildings
Transport

Foundation Themes
Homes

Neighbourhood number line

Group size
Up to six children.

What you need
Large sheets of paper; paint; paintbrushes; pens; card; textured paper and materials such as foil, bubble wrap, sandpaper, Cellophane and so on; familiar objects found in the setting and at home; table.

Preparation
Cut out card number shapes from 1 to 10 and cover them with a range of textured materials, so that you have a sandpaper number 1, a fur-covered number 2 and so on. Make large paper banner labels for ten local buildings or areas, such as the post office, library, park, fruit shop, shoe shop and so on.

What to do
Show the children the banner labels. Provide each child with a large sheet of paper and invite them to paint one of the buildings or areas on to it. When the paintings are dry, display them in a long line at child height, adding the corresponding banner label above each painting.

Look at the textured numbers together and choose one to go above each label. Then select items to go on a table, directly underneath the paintings. For example, if number 1 is the post office, find one envelope to place next to it; if a fruit shop is number 2, find two apples; select three balls for the park at number 3; and so on. When the display is complete, choose two numbers (to suit the ability of your group) and ask the children to gather the items from those numbers, for example, two apples and three balls, then count the total number of objects. Ask another child to return both apples to number 2 and the three balls to number 3. Continue until all the children have had a turn at returning the items to the correct numbers.

Support and extension
Invite younger children to find objects that match, for example, give them a ball and ask them to find another one. With older children, introduce two dice and ask them to throw these and match the numbers on the dice to numbers on the number line.

Home partnership
Ask parents and carers to contribute suitable objects, such as train tickets for the train station. Send home a number line and ask them to help their children to find these numbers at home, such as in the TV guide or on the telephone.

Further ideas
♦ Using play food in the home corner, give Teddy three buns and Dolly two biscuits, then count how many items there are all together.
♦ Invite the children to play 'Shop', counting money in two purses to see if there are enough pennies for the shopping.

Theme links
Buildings
Numbers

When I was small

Stepping Stone
Begin to differentiate between past and present.

Early Learning Goal
Find out about past and present events in their own lives, and in those of their families and other people they know.

Group size
Whole group.

What you need
Old-fashioned household items, such as kitchen utensils, items used for washing clothes, toys, old telephone, lamp or candlestick, clothes and so on; photographs and pictures in books of old-fashioned objects used in homes; pens; sheets of thin A4 card; camera, preferably Instamatic or digital so that the photographs are instantly available.

Preparation
Fold the A4 sheets of card in half and give one to each child.

What to do

Look at each of the items in turn, passing it around the group. Comment on the colour, shape and materials that the first item is made from. Does it look new or old? Who would have used it? What does it do? Make sure that all the children have time to explore the object. Ask open questions and make comments to encourage the children to suggest what it might be, passing the object around the group again. Do this for all the items.

Vary the game by describing one of the objects by its function, such as 'something for cleaning clothes', and asking which object it is and why.

Next, ask each child to draw one of the objects on the front of their card. Then photograph the object, mount the photo inside the card and label the object alongside it. Display all the cards so that the children can look at the drawings, peek inside the cards to see the photographs and match them to the objects.

Support and extension

Choose just two objects to show younger children. Compare old and new objects talking about their colour, feel and use. Take older children to visit an antique shop to find other interesting items from the past.

Home partnership

Invite families into your setting to show the children photos and mementoes from their home and childhood days.

Further ideas

♦ Look at old local photographs and compare them with how the area looks now.
♦ Ask a local antique dealer to bring in a few items to show the children. Find the equivalent new objects and compare the differences.
♦ Make a display of old teddy bears and toys belonging to staff and parents when they were children.

Theme links
Time
Toys

Foundation Themes
Homes

Around my neighbourhood

Group size
Up to eight children.

What you need
A4 paper; clipboard for each child; pens; wax crayons.

Preparation
Draw a circle, square, rectangle, triangle, oval and diamond on a sheet of paper. Photocopy it for each child. Attach each sheet and several more blank sheets of paper to each clipboard.

What to do

Look at the clipboard sheets with the children. Examine each shape and ask the children where they might see the shapes on homes, shops or in the park.

Next, take the children for a short walk around the neighbourhood, taking the clipboards with you. Look for the shapes, one at a time, trying to find them in nature as well as in manufactured objects. When you find a shape, such as a circular road sign, stop in a safe area and invite each child to draw the road sign in their circle. Continue finding each shape in turn, asking questions such as, 'Can you find an oval-shaped leaf?', and looking in every possible area or shop, such as the fruit shop to identify the shapes of the produce there.

Encourage the children to look at colours and textures as well, such as rectangular, red, rough bricks in a low wall, and to find objects of the same shape but different size, such as the round light on a bicycle lamp and the circle of a roundabout.

Support and extension

With younger children, play the game in your outdoor area. Ask older children to look at curves and corners, and also at patterns in nature, such as the soft-curved leaves, the straight lines of the wooden fence and the wobbly lines of the tree trunk.

Home partnership

Invite parents and carers to make the most of their journeys with their children. As they are out and about, encourage them to count how many circles they can find one day, how many rectangles the next day, how many squares the day after and so on.

Further ideas

♦ Take the children to visit an important building in your neighbourhood, for example, the post office, church or fire station. Encourage them to look at the big shapes, such as the steeple and the arches on the windows of the church, then look at the smaller shapes, such as the details on the door, or the pattern of the tiles on the floor or walls.
♦ Talk to the children about steep hills and flat roads and invite them to tell you whether their house is on a hill or in a flat area.

Theme links
My town
Shapes

Going on a journey

Stepping Stone
Demonstrate the control necessary to hold a shape or fixed position.

Early Learning Goal
Move with control and co-ordination.

Group size
Whole group.

What you need
Six sheets of A4 paper; marker pen; CD player and CD, or tape recorder and tape.

Preparation
Fold each sheet of paper in half and draw a symbol to represent the library, your setting, a café, a post office, the shops or a home inside each one.

What to do

This game is a variation on 'Musical statues', but the whole group remains in the game. Ask the children to stand in a wide space. Explain that you are going to play a listening game with some music, and that they will have to stand very still when it stops. Then tell them that when the music starts you will ask them to pretend to ride a bike, go for a walk, drive a bus and so on, as you are all going on a journey. Say that, first, you are going to a friend's house to ask if they want to play, and that you are going to walk to the bus stop.

Start the music and walk with the children slowly around the room. Remind them that they must listen carefully and stop moving when the music stops playing. Stop the music and make sure that all the children are standing still. Then continue the game, telling the children that you are going, for example, on the bus, on the train or running in the park.

When you have played the game several times, ask one of the children to choose a card and to tell you where you are all going next by looking at the symbol inside. Ask another child to say how you are going to travel, and start your journey. Do this for all the cards.

Support and extension

Play alongside younger children, holding hands and modelling the actions. Keep the game simple and brief. Invite older children to think of their own ideas for the journey, involving people who help us in the neighbourhood, such as the fire service or police officers.

Home partnership

Ask parents and carers to play a listening game with their children, pausing for a moment at home to see what they can hear.

Further ideas

♦ Read the story *We're Going on a Bear Hunt* by Michael Rosen (Walker Books). Invite the children to sing along and act it out, using a shaker to move them from one action to the next.
♦ Play a rowing game with the children sitting opposite each other in pairs. When they hear a tap on a drum, they must stop moving.

Theme links
Sound
Transport

Foundation
Themes
Homes

This is our town

Group size
Four children.

What you need
Flour; salt; water;
PVA glue; paint;
lolly sticks; simple
dough tools; rolling-
pins; ruler; baking
trays; blunt pencil;
ribbon; access to a
cooker.

Preparation
Make salt dough
using two cups of
flour, one cup of
salt and one cup of
water. Mix well and
knead for at least
five minutes.

What to do
Divide the dough among the children
and invite each child to roll it out.
Help them to cut a simple rectangle
shape, using the ruler and dough tools, and then to make a model of their home or
a local building, such as a block of flats, church or shop. With the lolly sticks and
dough tools, create brick patterns, windows and doors.

Allow the children plenty of time to make their buildings. If necessary, the dough
can be kneaded and rolled out again.

When the children have completed their buildings, make sure that they all wash
their hands in warm soapy water. Salt dough can be very drying and can irritate
young skin.

Make a hole with the end of a pencil at the top of each salt-dough plaque for
threading some ribbon through later. Bake the plaques at 100°C (200°F, Gas Mark
¼) for six to twelve hours. When the plaques are cool, invite the children to paint
them, then seal them with watered-down PVA glue. Thread some ribbon through
the hole in each plaque and hang all the plaques alongside each other to make a
street-scene display.

Support and extension
Help younger children to roll out the dough and use plastic bricks to print on their
dough buildings. Encourage older children to add more detail to their buildings
with collage materials after baking.

Home partnership
Ask parents and carers to bring in any pictures or photographs of local buildings
that they may have to add to the display. Put dough recipes on the parents' noticeboard for their information.

Further ideas
♦ Make a selection of sandwiches with the children, using a house-shaped cutter
and a range of fillings.
♦ Look at pictures that show buildings at night-time and invite the children to use
wet and dry chalks to draw their own buildings on black paper, splattering silver
paint to create the moon and stars.

Theme links
Buildings
Our town
Shapes

Foundation
Themes
Homes

Tiles and bricks

Stepping Stone
Use ideas involving fitting, overlapping and grids.

Early Learning Goal
Explore colour, texture, shape, form and space in two or three dimensions.

Group size
Four children.

What you need
Plastic bricks and other printing tools; paint; mixing palettes; collage materials, including corrugated card and coloured Cellophane; cardboard box for each child; glue scissors; sticky tape; thick paper.

Preparation
Borrow a selection of design and architecture books from a library, with photographs of buildings and parts of buildings that show, for example, brick patterns, stained-glass windows, roof tiles and so on. Pre-cut some of the collage materials into regular shapes.

What to do
Show the photographs to the children and talk about the colours, shapes and patterns that you can see. Match these to some of the collage materials.

Next, look at the printing tools and paints. Discuss how you can mix the paints to match the colours in the pictures, and how the printing tools can be used to create some of the effects and patterns that you can see. Ask the children to choose one of the pictures and to try to make a similar effect on thick paper using the printing and collage materials.

Now help each child to open out their cardboard box and turn it inside out to provide a fresh surface for their work. Give the children the pre-cut shapes and help them to look at how they can fit together to form patterns, for example, tiling or brick patterns.

Display the finished paintings and models next to the book pictures.

Support and extension
Give younger children a selection of pre-cut shapes, then take turns to add 'tiles' to make a roof, overlapping them and lining them up, and to add brick shapes to make a wall. Encourage older children to experiment with a wide variety of printing and collage materials.

Home partnership
Ask parents and carers to contribute any postcards, photographs or drawings of interesting buildings. Copy the rhyme 'A house of patterns' on the photocopiable sheet on page 85 and encourage the children and their families to decorate it with colourful shapes.

Further ideas
♦ Take the children for a walk to find patterns of overlapping shapes, for example, fencing or roof tiles. Then look at patterns in nature and use collected natural materials, such as fallen leaves, bark and twigs, in the sand tray for building and creating overlapping patterns.
♦ Look at mosaic patterns together and use pre-cut shapes or buttons to make mosaics around the theme of 'Homes'.

Theme links
Patterns
Shapes

Lights in the house

Group size
Up to eight children.

What you need
Familiar objects found in homes, including a torch, clock, blanket, key, television remote control and baby bath.

Preparation
Familiarise yourself with the tune of the song 'The Wheels on the Bus' (Traditional).

What to do
Sit in a circle and pass around the objects for the children to explore. Explain that together you are going to make up a new song about homes.
Begin by picking up the torch and sing, to the tune of 'The Wheels on the Bus':

The lights in the house go on and off
On and off, on and off,
The lights in the house go on and off
All day long.

Let each child, in turn, choose an object and, together, agree on the words to sing, such as, 'The clock in the kitchen goes, tick, tock, tick' (clock), 'The children in the bed go wriggle, wriggle, wriggle' (blanket) or 'The door to my flat goes open and closed' (key). Encourage the children to contribute their own ideas, take turns and listen carefully. Place each prop in a row and sing the song through, using the props as a reminder.

Support and extension
With younger children, choose familiar objects of particular significance to them, such as a spoon or toy, and sing, for example, 'The spoon in the bowl goes round and round' or 'The toy in the box come in and out'. Encourage older children to work in groups of three to create a new verse. Record their songs with a tape or video recorder.

Home partnership
Invite parents and carers to listen to their children singing the new songs. Make a list of favourite nursery songs, posting the words of some of them on the parents' noticeboard.

Further ideas
♦ Ask each child to bring an object from home that they can use to make a sound, then play a listening game to identify the different sounds.
♦ Use a set of pans and a variety of spoons or kitchen utensils and see how many different sounds the children can make. How can they change the sounds?

Theme links
Nursery rhymes
Sound

Chapter 4
Animal homes

Animals are a source of endless fascination for young children and provide excellent opportunities to learn more about the natural world. Activities about animal homes help children to consider the needs of others and develop a sense of responsibility in caring for animals as well as in the protection of their own environment

I live in the sea

Group size
Four to six children.

What you need
A copy of *The Rainbow Fish* by Marcus Pfister (North-South Books); two large sheets of paper; pens; crayons; scissors; glue; pictures of animals who live in the sea.

Preparation
Familiarise yourself with the story *The Rainbow Fish*. Draw a large outline of a rainbow fish on one sheet of paper and cut the second sheet into shapes to make scales for the rainbow fish.

What to do
Begin by looking at the pictures in *The Rainbow Fish* and ask each child to name a creature that lives in the sea. Read the book to the children and talk together about how the rainbow fish is feeling at different points in the story. Ask them to describe the rainbow fish's home, the plants, rocks, water and any other fish and sea creatures.

Next, encourage each child to draw one of the creatures or fish that share the rainbow fish's sea home on a paper scale. Write captions using the child's own words on each picture.

Stepping Stone
Have a positive self-image and show that they are comfortable with themselves.

Early Learning Goal
Understand that they can expect others to treat their needs, views, cultures and beliefs with respect.

Help each child to glue their scale on to the group's large rainbow fish shape. Display the collage next to the book and pictures of other creatures and fish that live in the sea.

Support and extension
Encourage younger children to sponge-paint sea colours on to their paper scales. Invite older children to copy the labels and captions that you have written on to a second scale and let them glue this next to their sea creature picture on the group rainbow fish.

Home partnership
Leave the *The Rainbow Fish* out for the children and their families to share. Place a small 'notes for parents' bookmark in the book, giving suggestions for things to talk about with their children. Invite parents and carers to bring in any books that they have about creatures that live in the sea, and display these alongside the rainbow fish, book and pictures.

Further ideas
♦ If possible, take the children on a visit to a local tropical-fish shop to look at all the different creatures. Compare the warm-water tropical tanks with the cold-seawater tanks.
♦ Provide a range of plastic sea creatures and shells, Cellophane seaweed and sand for water play around sea-creatures' homes.

Theme links
Animals and plants
Under the sea

My pet's home

Stepping Stone
Show care and concern for others, for living things and the environment.

Early Learning Goal
Consider the consequences of their words and actions for themselves and others.

Group size
Six children.

What you need
Picture books about pets; soft-toy pets; cat basket; fish tank; dog's bowl; sheets of thin card; hole-punch; ribbon; small sheets of plain paper; glue; crayons; scissors; magazines about pets; catalogues with pet-care items such as dog baskets.

Preparation
Draw an outline of a dog basket, cut it out and use it as a template to cut the same shape from each sheet of card. Using the scissors, hole-punch and ribbon, make a blank dog-basket-shaped album for the children to decorate.

What to do

Invite a parent or carer to bring their pet from home to show to the children. Check for any allergies. Talk about where the pet lives, how it is cared for, how it is kept warm and healthy, and how it gets food and water. Look at pictures of pets and the soft-toy pets, and discuss different pets' homes.

Next, invite each child to say if they have a pet, or to tell you about a pet that they may like to have one day, then encourage them to talk about their neighbours' or friends' pets.

As you talk, look at your selection of items, such as the cat basket and dog's bowl, and ask why each item is important and how it is used to care for a pet. Look through the pet pictures again and ask each child to cut out or draw a picture of a pet. Then help them to cut out or draw the items that the pet would need for their home, such as food, a blanket for warmth, toys and so on. Finally, paste each picture into the pet album.

Support and extension

Help younger children to tear pictures of pets to paste to the front cover of the album. Encourage older children to make a word or picture shopping list of all the things that they would need to care for their pets.

Home partnership

Invite parents and carers to bring in photographs of their or other people's pets. Display them and add captions around them to encourage the children and their families to talk together about the pets, with questions such as 'Which is the smallest pet?', 'Can you find the brown hamster?' and so on.

Further ideas

◆ Read the story *The Great Pet Sale* by Mick Inkpen (Hodder).
◆ Add toy cats and dogs, baskets, blankets, bowls and so on to the home corner.

Theme links
Food
Pets

In the rainforest

Stepping Stone
Know information can be
relayed in the form of print

Early Learning Goal
Explore and experiment with
sounds, words and texts.

Group size
Four to six children.

What you need
A large sheet of card; chopped bark; peat; grass cuttings; twigs; leaves; glue; sponge-painting equipment; books and magazines about the rainforest; scissors; toy animals; marker pen and large sheets of paper, or a computer and printer; the finger rhyme 'I Saw a Slippery, Slithery Snake' from *This Little Puffin...* compiled by Elizabeth Matterson (Puffin Books).

Preparation
Familiarise yourself with the rhyme.

What to do

Look at the pictures of the rainforest in the books and magazines with the children, and explain to them that the rainforest is home to many creatures. Talk about the darkness under the trees, the heat and the rain. Help the children to think about the different parts of the rainforest, such as the forest floor, the leaves and branches of the bushes, the canopy or roof of the rainforest (the tops of tall trees) and the rivers. Then look at the pictures again and talk about each creature and where it might live in the rainforest, such as butterflies, birds and minibeasts.

Do the finger rhyme with the children, encouraging them to join in with the words and actions. Then cut pictures of rainforest animals from the magazines and help the children to make a rainforest on the large sheet of card. Use the natural materials and sponge-painting equipment to create a rainforest with rivers, a forest floor (bark and peat) and a canopy (twigs and leaves). Make it dark and very dense, then add the magazine pictures of rainforest creatures.

Display the finished collage, along with a written or typed-out version of the finger rhyme and the toy animals.

Support and extension

With younger children, do the finger rhyme on a one-to-one basis, helping them to copy your actions. Encourage older children to add a steam-and-rain effect to the rainforest collage by bubble-painting grey or white paint.

Home partnership

Invite parents and carers to sing the song 'Row, Row, Row Your Boat' (Traditional) with their children. Put the words and actions on the parents' noticeboard as a reminder, including a final verse about meeting a crocodile!

Further ideas

♦ Use the same techniques and materials to produce an underwater scene or a jungle scene.
♦ Make rainforest birds with brightly coloured feathers and glittery collage materials.

Theme links
Around the world
The rainforest

Foundation
Themes
Homes

What happened next?

Group size
Four children.

What you need
A copy of the story
After the Storm by
Nick Butterworth
(Picture Lions);
empty sand tray
or similar; branch
that fits in the tray;
play people; toy
animals; miniature
wheelbarrow or
trailer; wooden
building blocks;
lolly sticks; lengths
of string; acorns;
warm hat and scarf.

Preparation
Familiarise yourself
with the story and
so that you are
ready to tell it to
the children using
some of the props
above.

What to do
Sit on the floor with the children and say that you are a character from a favourite story-book and that you are going to tell them a tale. Put on the hat and scarf and introduce yourself as Percy the Park Keeper. Using your own words, tell the story of *After the Storm*, using some of the props to help to keep the children's attention, such as the miniature wheelbarrow and the acorns.

When you have finished telling the story, show the children the story-book and talk about the title pages, the illustrations and the final illustration of the tree home. Ask them to tell you about their favourite part of the story. Read the book again, pausing to focus on how the animals are working together to build a new home to keep safe and warm.

Next, help the children to set up the story scene in the empty sand tray. Play alongside them, providing a commentary to help them to sequence their play to match the story-line. Gradually step back and allow them to play freely, building a new home for the animals.

Support and extension
With younger children, share the book on a one-to-one basis, encouraging them to turn the pages and look for details in the pictures. Invite older children to work together co-operatively to build a new home for the park animals.

Home partnership
Put up a list of favourite story-books and encourage parents and carers to add their children's favourites from home to the list. Include details of your local library's opening times on the parents' noticeboard.

Further ideas
♦ Ask your local librarian to visit and bring in a selection of story-books, information books, picture books and poetry and rhyme books.
♦ Help each child to make a bookmark on which to list any books that they borrow from the setting.

Theme links
Animals
Stories and rhymes

Spider's web

Group size
Four children.

What you need
The rhyme 'Spider, spider, spins all day' on the photocopiable sheet on page 85; books about spiders; pictures of spiders' webs; corrugated card; small pieces of smooth wood; strong glue; child's hammer; flat-head wood tacks; plastic bottle tops; cotton reels; thick straws; small wooden sticks and blocks; lolly sticks; silver-coloured gift ribbon; wool; thin string; ribbon; black and white paints; sponges; paintbrushes.

Preparation
Make sure that all the wood items are smooth and splinter-free.

Theme links
Minibeasts
Nursery rhymes

What to do
Look at the pictures of spiders and talk about a spider's web as the spider's home and as a food trap. Read and talk about the rhyme on the photocopiable sheet. If possible, take the children outdoors to hunt for spiders' webs, looking at their colours and shapes and talking about how spiders spin them.

Back inside, help each child to choose materials to build their own spider's web. Use either corrugated card or flat pieces of smooth wood as base boards. Encourage the children to use a range of methods for fixing posts to the base boards to wind the threads around. For example, they could glue or hammer the wood blocks or tacks, or poke some of the items through the corrugated card. Take extra care with all the woodwork tools and never leave the children unattended with them. Ensure that the children are aware of the potential dangers and are clear about the safe use of the tools.

Next, encourage the children to make their webs. Provide a variety of threads and comment with each child on the different patterns that they make. Allow plenty of uninterrupted time to ensure that the children can try out their ideas and different ways of making the webs, helping them to sponge or splatter-paint their webs, mixing the black and white paints to make a range of colours and effects.

Support and extension
With younger children, prepare the wooden posts ready for threading and sing the finger rhyme 'Incy Wincy Spider' (Traditional) as they make their webs. Encourage older children to use painting and collage materials to make a spider for their web.

Home partnership
Give parents and carers a sheet of paper with three interesting facts about spiders to talk about with their children, as well as the words and actions for the traditional rhyme 'Incy, Wincy Spider'.

Further ideas
♦ Use thick card and a hole-punch to make spider's-web cards, threading with wool.
♦ Learn together the rhyme 'I Have a Little Spider' from *This Little Puffin...* compiled by Elizabeth Matterson (Puffin Books).

How many do you see?

Stepping Stone
Select the correct numeral to represent 1 to 5, then 1 to 9, objects.

Early Learning Goal
Count reliably up to 10 everyday objects.

Group size
Five children.

What you need
The photocopiable sheet 'Animal cards' on page 95; sheet of thin A4 card; scissors; pens.

Preparation
Divide the sheet of thin card into ten sections (each approximately 10cm by 6cm). Cut out the sections into cards and write a numeral from 1 to 10 on each card. Make a copy of the photocopiable sheet on to thin card and cut out the pictures.

What to do
Help the children to sort the cards into two piles: a number pile and an animal pile. Look at each of the animal cards and talk about the animals and their homes. Shuffle the animal cards and place them all face down in a pile in the middle of the table, then spread the number cards face up around them. To play the game, ask the youngest child to take the first animal card from the pile, and help them to count how many animals there are in their home and to find the matching number card from the table. Continue to play until you have gone through all the animal cards, asking the children to take turns to count and match the animals to the numbers.

When all the cards have been matched, explain to the children that you are going to sing the song 'Old Macdonald Had a Farm' (Traditional) and that they should each, in turn, choose one of their cards as the centre of the verse, for example:

Old Macdonald had a farm,
E-I-E-I-O!
And on that farm he had six pigs,
E-I-E-I-O!

Support and extension
For younger children, play the game with toy farm animals. Provide older children with blank cards for them to add their own animals in homes and matching number cards.

Home partnership
Let the children take home the cards to play the game with their families.

Further ideas
♦ Encourage the children to think of animals that have two legs, four legs, then six, eight or more legs, talking about where each animal lives.
♦ Make cards with different animals in homes and play a 'Beetle drive' game.

Theme links
Animals
Numbers

Build a nest

Stepping Stone
Comment and ask questions about where they live and the natural world.

Early Learning Goal
Observe, find out about and identify features in the place they live and the natural world.

Group size
Up to six children.

What you need
Books and pictures about birds, bird boxes and nests; children's binoculars; bird boxes; old nests; large, strong cardboard box; shoeboxes; straw; twigs; leaves; moss; scissors; modelling clay or play dough; paint; paintbrushes; glue; string; collage materials.

Preparation
Cut pieces of thick card, approximately 60cm x 15cm, from the large cardboard box.

What to do
Show the children the books and pictures and talk about where birds live and how they build their homes. Look at the bird boxes and nests, and invite the children to tell you where they might find these. Ask them why birds build nests in trees, then talk about the nesting materials and different sizes of nests.

Examine the bird boxes again, paying attention to their shape and how they are made. What do the children think will be inside them?

Next, help each child to build a bird box or a nest. For a bird box, either use a shoebox or the pieces of thick card, bending the card to make the middle of the box and the rest of the card to make the base and lid, using sticky tape to hold it together. For a nest, use a shoebox and build the nest in it by weaving together the twigs and adding moss and leaves.

Encourage the children to use a wide range of natural materials and paint to create the shapes and textures that they have seen in the pictures, and to use the clay or play dough to make eggs for their nests.

Support and extension
Work alongside younger children, helping them to choose appropriate materials. Ask older children to look through the books and to each choose the bird who will live in their nest. Help them to make labels for their nests.

Home partnership
Ask parents and carers to bring in bird boxes or other resources to support this activity and to help their children to collect natural materials to bring along too.

Further ideas
♦ Invite a bird-watcher to visit your setting and bring in books, photographs, binoculars and bird-watching equipment. Talk about the places that they have visited and the different nests that they have seen.
♦ Make pictures of the different animal homes, pets and wildlife in your neighbourhood, such as dogs in kennels, birds in nests and ducks in ponds.

Theme links
Animals
In the air

Foundation
Themes
Homes

My shell is my home

Group size
Four children.

What you need
Paint; cup of dry sand; feathers; sticks; rollers; different-sized paintbrushes; printing materials; thick card; scissors; cotton buds; plastic forks; sea shells; coloured paper; books and pictures about creatures that live in shells, such as snails, hermit crabs, tortoises, turtles and terrapins, mussels, whelks and so on.

What to do
Invite a parent or carer, or someone from the local pet shop to bring a tortoise, turtle or terrapin to your setting. Go to the supermarket or fish stall and buy some crabs, whelks, mussels and other creatures that live in shells. Hunt for snails in the garden, and make some paint combs by cutting patterns along the edges of pieces of thick card.

Very carefully, show the children all the different creatures and explain that for each one their home is their shell. Feel the sea shells and discuss their textures and patterns. Ask the children questions such as, 'What shapes can you see?' and 'How many spirals can you find?'. Talk about how the shell makes a good home for these creatures. Invite each child to choose some shells and patterns and to try to make similar patterns on a sheet of paper.

Play alongside the children, trying out different painting tools, such as the feathers and cotton buds. Print patterns to make a tortoise's shell, or create the spirals that you see on the sea shells. Try the paint combs to spread paint thinly, perhaps sprinkling it to make a textured finish.

Support and extension
With younger children, choose just one pattern, such as the spiral, and help them to make lots of spirals using the different tools. Encourage older children to make their own paint combs to achieve different effects.

Home partnership
Invite parents and carers to work alongside their children to create their own shell patterns.

Further ideas
◆ Read the rhyme 'A Hive for a Honey-bee' from *This Little Puffin...* compiled by Elizabeth Matterson (Puffin Books) and ask the children to build or make one of the animal homes from the rhyme. Help each child to select the most appropriate materials, for example, clay, bricks, box modelling or collage materials, to build their animal homes.
◆ Use hardening dough to make homes for toy animals.
◆ Read *The Tale of a Snail* by Judith Nicholls (Ladybird Books).

Theme links
Animals
Under the sea

In a burrow

Stepping Stone
Experiment with different ways of moving.

Early Learning Goal
Move with confidence, imagination and in safety.

Group size
Up to eight children.

What you need
Books and pictures about animals; large sheet of paper; marker pen; blankets; large cardboard boxes; tunnel; camera or video camera, if available.

What to do

Spread out the blankets, cardboard boxes and tunnel on the floor, making sure that there is space for the children to move safely between them. Secure the edges of the blankets and remember to look out for potential trip hazards.

Look at the pictures and books and help the children to find animals that live in burrows. Make a picture list of the animals, such as rabbits, snakes, worms, badgers and moles, using words and making a simple line drawing of each animal. Talk about and name their home and how the animal might move getting into and out of it, such as worms wriggling, moles digging, rabbits hopping and so on.

Next, discuss which animal makes a burrow and how animals that live in burrows might find their way around and in and out of their homes. How do they know which hole is their own?

Now play a game in which you call out the name of an animal from the list and the children move like that animal until they hear you whisper, 'Stop hopping, bunnies!' or 'Stop slithering, snakes!' and so on. Record the children's actions using a camera or video camera if you have one. Encourage the children to use a range of large and small movements and to move in and around the blankets, boxes and tunnel carefully. If you have taken photographs, display them alongside the pictures and books about animals in burrows and the picture list.

Support and extension

Help younger children to imitate your actions. Invite older children to take turns to choose an animal from the picture list and move like it.

Home partnership

Suggest that parents and carers take their children to parks or soft-play areas to give them the opportunity to move in a variety of ways.

Further ideas

♦ Make burrows in the wet-sand tray and use cardboard tubes, toy animals and lengths of thick cord as pretend worms.
♦ Read story-books about different animal homes to the children and talk about them together.

Theme links
Animals
Underground

Where do I live?

Stepping Stone
Use increasing control over an object by touching, pushing, patting, throwing, catching or kicking it.

Early Learning Goal
Use a range of small and large equipment.

Group size
Up to six children.

What you need
Large and small balls; beanbags; quoits; blue mat or blanket; play tunnel or large cardboard box; green fabric or paper; bubble wrap; green hoop; sticky tape; scissors; pens; thin card.

What to do

Label the blue mat or blanket as 'sea', with words and a picture symbol, such as waves. Similarly, label the tunnel as 'underground', the green fabric or paper as 'forest', the bubble wrap as 'ice and snow' and the green hoop as 'farm'. Spread these items out in an area. Make simple line drawings of three animals that make their homes in each of these places. Draw one animal per card and fix each card to a ball, quoit or beanbag with sticky tape.

Roll or throw a ball, beanbag or quoit to the first child. Encourage them to use two hands to catch it and to look at it carefully. Ask the child to name the animal and say where it lives – for example, if the label shows a picture of a fish, its home is the sea.

Next, ask the child to carefully roll, push or throw the ball, beanbag or quoit to the correct area, such as the blue mat or blanket for the fish. If they miss or are wrong, encourage them to continue trying until the ball, beanbag or quoit is in the correct area.

Let each child have a turn until all the animals are in the correct homes.

Support and extension

Younger children may find it easier if you roll the smallest ball to them. Encourage older children to work in pairs, with one child choosing the ball, beanbag or quoit and throwing it to their partner, who then throws it at the target.

Home partnership

Leave out the equipment for this activity and invite parents and carers to try it with their children. Also encourage them to play a variety of ball games with their children to develop accurate throwing, catching and rolling.

Theme links
Movement
Shapes

Further ideas

♦ Half-fill balloons with warm water and let the children take it in turns to throw them into hoops on the floor outside.
♦ Provide a wide range of equipment for the children to practise rolling, catching and throwing, including beach balls, rolled-up socks and foam balls.
♦ Ask the children to stand in a circle and gently throw a beanbag to each other. See how far they can go around the circle without dropping it.

Safe in my cocoon

Stepping Stone
Begin to use representation as a means of communication.

Early Learning Goal
Respond in a variety of ways to what we see, hear, smell, touch and feel.

Group size
Up to eight children.

What you need
A copy of the story *The Crunching Munching Caterpillar* by Sheridan Cain (Little Tiger Press); ribbons; bubble wrap; foil; Cellophane; net fabric; silky scarves; large sheets of corrugated card or large cardboard boxes; blankets; scissors; tape recorder or CD player; tape or CD of soft music.

What to do
Cut the bubble wrap, Cellophane and foil into long strips to make streamers.

Read the story to the children and talk about how the caterpillar lives on leaves and then builds a special home called the cocoon. Explain to the children that this is its home for just a short time: the caterpillar soon changes into a butterfly, the air becomes its new home and it feeds on flowers. Talk about how the caterpillar might move, slowly wriggling around leaves, crawling into the cocoon that it has built and then emerging as a butterfly, flitting about quickly.

Next, explain to the children that you are going to retell the story and play some music, and that as they listen to each part of the story, they should try to act it out, first being the caterpillar crawling, then the caterpillar curled up in a cocoon and finally the butterfly. Tell the story slowly, stopping regularly so that the children can think about how they might move and which props they may wish to use. For example, the sheets of corrugated card or cardboard boxes and blankets can be cocoons for the children to curl up inside, and the streamers can be their wings as they dance about like butterflies. As you pause in the storytelling, play the music to allow unhurried time for the children to develop their actions and ideas.

Support and extension
Join in with younger children, making the story as simple as possible and asking them to copy your actions. Leave the materials and tape recorder or CD player out for older children to work out their own ideas and make up stories about caterpillars and butterflies.

Home partnership
Invite parents and carers to come to watch the children's actions and dance as you read the story.

Further ideas
♦ Look at some beautiful butterfly pictures, then let the children to mix their own paint colours, dropping and splattering them on to blotting paper.
♦ Collect some caterpillars and look at them with magnifying glasses or bug-viewers. List all the words that the children use to describe the caterpillars, grouping together those that rhyme.

Theme links
Changes
Minibeasts

Foundation **Themes**
Homes

Dolphin music

Group size
Six children.

What you need
Pictures of dolphins; tape recorder or CD player; tape or CD of dolphin sounds (widely available from high-street music stores or online from Amazon); musical instruments, real and improvised, metal and wooden, such as different packets for shakers, boxes, wooden bricks, tins and pans, with a selection of beaters.

What to do

Make sure that all the improvised sound-makers are safe and suitable for the purpose. Then ask the children to lie quietly on the carpet with their eyes closed. Listen to the music together and ask the children if they have any ideas about what the sounds are. Encourage them to describe these, giving them clues, such as, 'The sounds come from an animal at home in the deep oceans'. Show them the pictures of the dolphins and explain that families of dolphins live together, swimming through the oceans and looking for food. Talk about other animals who have the ocean as their home, such as whales, octopuses, fish and so on.

Next, ask each child to choose an instrument and see if they can make a similar sound to the 'clicks' of the dolphin. Take it in turns, talking about the sounds that the instrument makes. Help the children to experiment with the sounds, brushing instead of tapping, rubbing instruments with beaters, using different beaters, holding shakers in different ways and so on.

Let the children look around the setting to find other improvised instruments that might make similar sounds. Stop and listen to the tape frequently throughout the activity, talking about the sounds, commenting and prompting suggestions about how similar sounds might be made.

Support and extension

Allow younger children freedom to explore just a few instruments. Ask older children to listen to and copy patterns of taps, squeaks and clicks.

Home partnership

Encourage parents and carers to contribute pictures of animals that live in the ocean as well as suitable resources for making simple sound-makers. Lend them the tape or CD of the dolphin sounds to listen to with their children at home.

Further ideas

♦ Use plastic and cardboard tubes of different lengths filled with a variety of grains and pulses to make different rainmakers.
♦ Try out the different sounds that you can make with water, adding plastic bottles, jugs, sieves and different beaters to the water tray.

Theme links
Sounds
Under the sea

Chapter 5

Unusual homes

As children's confidence grows, they become increasingly aware of the wider world in which they live. Extend their knowledge of different countries, cultures and communities with the following activities. This focus on unusual homes provides opportunities for the children to develop their creativity and imagination, and to understand and respect other people.

Around the world

Group size
Four children.

What you need
Pictures of homes around the world; large sheet of paper; catalogues and magazines; scissors; ruler; glue; pens; crayons.

What to do
Look at the pictures of different homes around the world. Notice similarities and differences in building materials, shapes, rooms, who might live there and how the homes are used. Then talk about homes in cities and rural areas in a variety of climates and discuss the differences.

Stepping Stone
Initiate interactions with other people.

Early Learning Goal
Have a developing respect for their own cultures and beliefs and those of other people.

Next, encourage the children to choose one of the homes. Explain that you are going to make a plan of the home so that you can tell the rest of the group about it. Ask the children to list the rooms. Agree on which room is going to be the biggest and draw an outline of this room on the large sheet of paper. Help the children to draw, or cut out from magazines, objects for this room, such as cooking pots for a kitchen. Continue adding different rooms, agreeing together on which rooms to draw next and discussing the different building materials, such as brick, mud, glass or wood.

Invite the children to draw the outside of the home, helping them to add pictures, symbols or words as labels. Show the plan to the rest of the group at circle time and explain how you worked together to make the plan.

Support and extension
Ask younger children to find real objects from around your setting for each room on the plan, such as a blanket for the sleeping area or a toy kettle for the kitchen. Encourage older children to think about how the people live in this home, adding these people's pictures and names.

Home partnership
Ask parents and carers to provide resources to support this activity, for example, photographs of, or objects from homes of family or friends who live in a different part of the world.

Further ideas
♦ Look on a globe at various parts of the world and talk about the different climates and homes, such as in icy places, deserts and so on.
♦ Build up a collection of play food and cooking utensils from around the world and talk about how we may cook and eat differently in different homes.

Theme links
Around the world
Buildings

Foundation Themes
Homes

If I lived here

Stepping Stone
Show confidence in linking up with others for support and guidance.

Early Learning Goal
Maintain attention, concentrate, and sit quietly when appropriate.

Group size
Four children.

What you need
Pictures of unusual homes such as castles, house boats, lighthouses, caravans, tents, skyscrapers, farmhouses and so on.

Preparation
Spread out the pictures on the floor.

What to do
Sit on the floor with the children and spend a few minutes looking together at the pictures. Talk about what it might be like to live in these homes. Find out about the children's experiences. Have any of them visited a castle or been on a house boat?

Next, choose one of the pictures and say, 'If I lived here I would...'. Complete the sentence with an appropriate phrase. For example, for the castle picture, say, 'I would sleep in the tower'. Then pass your picture to the child next to you and prompt them to complete the phrase, 'If I lived here...'. Pass the picture around until everyone has had a turn. Continue to play this game, encouraging the children to think about the unusual homes and add their own ideas and comments about what they would do if they lived there. Finish by asking each child to choose their favourite unusual home and to show this to the rest of the group.

Support and extension
Help younger children to choose one picture and ask them to find details in the picture, saying, for example, 'Let's find the chimney'. Challenge older children by asking them to remember the other children's comments, such as, 'If Laura lived here, she would sleep in the tower; what about Zach? What would he do?'.

Home partnership
Ask parents and carers to look out for unusual homes as they travel about with their children. Encourage them to provide pictures of castles, lighthouses, canal boats, caravans and so on.

Further ideas
♦ Build a castle with building bricks in an empty water tray. Use stickers and collage materials to add flags to the castle. Add play people and animals and water for the moat. Can you build a bridge across the moat?
♦ Create a junk model lighthouse, using foil for the signal light. Mount it on a rock and create a bubble print sea around it.

Theme links
Buildings
Water

Lighthouse life

Group size
Up to six children.

What you need
A copy of the story *The Lighthouse Keeper's Lunch* by Ronda Armitage (Scholastic); ball of string or ribbon; two strong card tubes; scissors; sticky tape; six bulldog clips; small pieces of paper; coloured pens.

Preparation
Carefully cut a deep, V-shaped groove at the top of each card tube. Familiarise yourself with the story-book.

What to do
Read the story to the children, then go back through the book looking at the pictures and retelling the story in your own words. Focus on the pulley system used to send the basket to the lighthouse keeper. Ask the children how the pulley might work and what it could be made of.

Next, give each child a piece of paper and some coloured pens to draw a picnic for the lighthouse keeper. Explain to the group that you are going to make a pulley to send the pictures across to the home corner. Show the children your selection of resources and ask them for ideas on how you could build the pulley. Look at the grooves in the tubes – what do they think they are for?

Fix one of the tubes to a wall opposite the home corner at a safe height for the children, above their heads so that they do not walk into the pulley system, but within easy reach with outstretched arms. Fix the second tube to the wall in the home corner, at the same height. Cut a length of string or ribbon to reach from one tube to the other and back again. Thread the bulldog clips on to the string, then stretch the string between the tubes, resting it in the V-shaped grooves and tying the ends together. This will create a simple pulley system. Tape the bulldog clips in place on the string and show the children how to clip their pictures on them and pull the string to send the pictures to the home corner.

Support and extension
Help younger children with mark-making and fix their pictures with simple push-on wooden clothes pegs. Encourage older children to write messages to send across to their friends.

Home partnership
Ask parents and carers to write messages to send to their children across the pulley system.

Further ideas
♦ Invite the children to build a lighthouse with construction bricks and use it in the water tray with boats and play people.
♦ Talk to the children about what it might be like to live in a lighthouse.

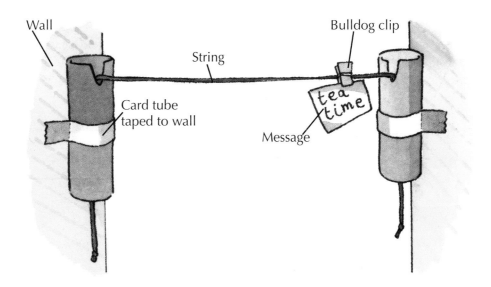

Wall
String
Bulldog clip
Card tube taped to wall
Message
tea time

Where is the mouse?

Group size
Up to six children.

What you need
A copy of the story *A Dark, Dark Tale* by Ruth Brown (Red Fox); black sugar paper; chalks; scissors; hole-punch; ribbon.

Preparation
Cut the sugar paper into several A4-size sheets (approximately 30cm x 20cm), so that there are two or three sheets for each child. Familiarise yourself with the story-book.

What to do
Read the story to the children, then look at the title and find the author's name on the front cover and the title page inside the book. Talk about how the story starts outside the dark house, in the dark wood, and slowly gets closer and closer to the mouse. Ask the children to talk about how they feel about the book. Is it scary? What makes it scary – the pictures, or maybe the words? What did they think was going to be in the box? How did they feel when they saw the mouse's home? What would it be like to live in the dark house? Do they think that the mouse likes his home? Look at the details in the pictures. Can the children spot other creatures who live in the dark wood?

Next, help the children to fold two or three sheets of black paper in half to make their own books. Use the hole-punch and ribbon to secure the pages. Then ask each child to create their own 'dark, dark tale'. Who will they hide in their box? Will it be a mouse? Use the chalks, either dry or, for deeper colours and different effects, dipped in water. Display the completed books alongside the story-book.

Support and extension
With younger children, tell the story to just two children at a time. Encourage older children to each copy or write their own title for their book, adding their name as author and illustrator.

Home partnership
Ask parents and carers who have a pet mouse to bring it into your setting to show the children. Make sure that the story-book is readily available and encourage the children to share it with their families at home.

Further ideas
♦ Use a dark sheet and large boxes to create a dark tunnel and tent to explore with torches. Fix brightly coloured objects and shiny shapes to the inside.
♦ Set up a dark corner and create shadows by shining the beams of torches through different objects.

Theme links
Animals
Light and dark

Tall, tall, tall

Group size
Four children.

What you need
Pictures of tall buildings; blank labels; pens; number line; different types of building bricks and blocks; recyclable model materials, including cardboard boxes; scissors; glue.

Preparation
Turn some of the cardboard boxes inside out and reassemble them to provide a plain outer surface.

What to do

Look at the pictures of the tall buildings and talk about what it might be like to live in a tall building. Talk about stairs and lifts, going shopping, playing outside, deliveries of letters and parcels and so on. Count the number of floors on some of the buildings, then look at the shapes, windows and doors.

Next, talk about neighbours and ask the children whether any of them live in a tall building or visit friends who do. Then encourage the children to create tower blocks with the different building blocks and recyclable materials, and to label each floor with a number, using the number line for guidance. Help the children with their constructions and make sure that each child holds their pen effectively when mark-making or writing the number labels.

Now look at the models one by one and guess with the children how many floors there are on each one. Talk about which is the tallest building, finding out which building has the most floors, and order the models by height.

Support and extension

Mark the numbers on the labels for younger children. When counting the completed models, count with the children, making sure that they place their finger on each floor as they count. Ask older children to measure the buildings that they have made, using hand spans or cutting lengths of ribbon the same height as the towers.

Home partnership

Give each child a picture of a tall building and ask them to colour it at home, and count the floors with their families. Invite parents and carers to look out for, and talk about local tall buildings with their children.

Further ideas

♦ Sing the song 'See that tall building' on the photocopiable sheet on page 88 with the children.
♦ Take the children to visit a local block of flats. Look at the shapes, floor numbers, flat numbers and so on. Travel in the lift and count the floors, or go up a flight of stairs and count the number of stairs.

Theme links
Buildings
Numbers

A very unusual home!

Group size
Four children.

What you need
The photocopiable sheet 'House game' on page 96; dice; five pieces of paper; coloured pens.

Preparation
Make a copy of the game on the photocopiable sheet.

What to do
Give each child and yourself a sheet of paper and pen. Explain that you are going to create some very unusual houses by throwing the dice, matching the number of spots on the dice to the correct number on the photocopiable sheet and drawing the corresponding item. Invite the first child to play, helping them to match the spots to a number on the sheet and letting them draw the picture. Continue to play, asking the children to take it in turns to throw the dice, match the numbers and draw. As each home grows, start to comment on the number of windows, doors and so on, and on how unusual these homes look.

After a few turns, ask each child to tell you the number that is after the number that they have thrown. For example, if the face with two spots is shown, they should say that the next number is 3. If they answer correctly, they can have an extra turn. Prompt each child to ensure that all the children are successful, in time, at getting an extra turn.

When the homes are complete (every home has at least one of each of the six items), let each child choose and write a house number on their unusual home.

Support and extension
For younger children, add a picture of the corresponding spotted dice face underneath each number. Challenge older children to name the number before, as well as the number after, the number that they have thrown.

Home partnership
Make a 'How to play this game' sheet for each child to take home to share with their families. Include instructions on how to make a number spinner, or number cards to turn over, just in case there is not a dice available at home.

Further ideas
♦ Invite the children to work together in the sand to build an unusual home, using materials such as wood, corks, shells, twigs, plastic cartons and foil.
♦ With the children, choose an unusual home, such as a house boat, castle or windmill, and build a pretend one as a den for imaginative play, either outside or in the home corner, involving the children in choosing simple props.

Theme links
Buildings
Numbers

Foundation Themes
Homes

Build a castle

Stepping Stone
Construct with a purpose in mind, using a variety of resources.

Early Learning Goal
Build and construct with a wide range of objects, selecting appropriate resources and adapting their work where necessary.

Group size
Up to six children.

What you need
Large cardboard boxes; corrugated card; length of card; large card tubes; sheets of fabric; scissors; string; marker pen; large sheet of paper; coloured Cellophane; glue; sticky tape; ribbon; hole-punch; paint; large paintbrushes and sponges; pictures of castles.

What to do

Look at the castle pictures and make a list, using pictures and words, of the main parts of the castle that you want to build on a large sheet of paper. Think about the shapes of the windows and whether they will have glass or be open. Then talk about turrets and battlements and decide whether the castle will have gates, or perhaps a portcullis and a drawbridge.

Build your castle together, using the large boxes and corrugated card for the walls. Help the children to paint, stipple or sponge-paint the walls. Use the marker pen to draw the windows, then carefully cut them out, covering them with Cellophane if you want a glass effect. Mark on battlements and use the tubes as turrets. Make a gateway between two of the boxes and create a portcullis by cutting equal lengths of ribbon, taping them to a length of card and fixing this over the entrance to the castle.

To make a drawbridge, open out one of the cardboard boxes and tape string to the corner of one of the flaps. Thread the string through a hole in the other corner, so that when the string is pulled, the flap lifts to close the drawbridge. Use the sheets of fabric to add a roof.

Finally, look at your original list and check that you have built all the main parts of your castle.

Support and extension

Help younger children to focus on building just one part of the castle. Encourage older children to each draw a plan of their castle, adding labels to show the different parts.

Home partnership

Provide parents and carers with ideas for building dens with their children, using items that are found in their homes.

Further ideas

♦ Make a castle play scene with wooden bricks and play people in the construction area.
♦ Use clay and similar materials to make castle shapes, such as battlements, slit windows and so on.

Theme links
Castles
Shapes

House boats

Stepping Stone
Show an interest in why things happen and how things work.

Early Learning Goal
Look closely at similarities, differences, patterns and change.

Group size
Four children.

What you need
Pictures and stories about house boats, perhaps including the popular children's television characters Rosie and Jim (Ragdoll Limited); four shallow trays as individual water trays; pebbles; corks; play people; lolly sticks; balsa wood; polystyrene; clean plastic cartons; glue; collage materials.

Preparation
Cut the balsa wood and polystyrene into small lengths. Check all resources for splinters and other hazards.

What to do
Look at the pictures and stories and discuss what it would be like to live on a house boat. First, talk about modern house boats, then old house boats and how people used to travel in them, taking coal and other goods between towns and cities. Think about what daily life is like on a house boat, where people cook, sleep, play and so on.

Next, help each child to build a house boat for their water tray, gluing together the different materials. Carry out a 'Floating or sinking?' activity with different items in turn, for example, the play people, the pebbles and the corks. Try floating the corks on their own, then on the boats, and do the same with the pebbles. Each time, encourage the children to say whether the boats are sinking or floating. Ask open questions and make comments on what is happening, and encourage the children to answer questions starting with, 'What do you think might happen if…?'. Encourage the children to test out their ideas and adapt their house boats as their ideas change.

Finally, help them to use the collage materials to decorate their house boats.

Support and extension
Make different boats for younger children and allow them to discover what will make them sink or float. Ask older children to use plastic bricks to build tunnels for their house boats to go through and encourage them to talk about them.

Home partnership
Provide parents and carers with pages from canal-holiday brochures and ask them to carry out cutting and sticking activities with their children at home.

Further ideas
♦ Decorate some flower pots with black shiny paint and let the children paint brightly coloured flowers on them in the style of canal-boat art.
♦ Use lengths of guttering on the floor outside, together with plastic boats and play people, to encourage canal play.

Theme links
Floating and sinking
Water

Living on a farm

Stepping Stone
Judge body space in relation to spaces available when fitting into confined spaces or negotiating holes and boundaries.

Early Learning Goal
Show awareness of space, of themselves and of others.

Group size
Whole group.

What you need
A play parachute or sheet; two egg-boxes; 12 plastic eggs or small balls; two small steering wheels or rings; white fabric; scissors; four brown ribbons; sticky tape.

Preparation
Cut the white fabric into four squares.

What to do

Spread out the parachute on the floor and ask the children to sit around the edge. Talk about living on a farm, mentioning different farms, such as those growing crops and those raising animals, and encourage the children to think about what it might be like to live in a farmhouse. Then stand up with the children and lift the parachute, stretching it out across your circle.

Next, throw the eggs or balls under the parachute. Ask two children to collect them in the egg-boxes while the rest of the group sings a verse of 'Old MacDonald Had a Farm' (Traditional), using the word 'hens' instead of 'cows'.

Now give the steering wheels or rings to two children and explain that they should pretend to be driving tractors under the parachute. Hold it high, then lower it gradually as you sing more of 'Old MacDonald Had a Farm', this time using the word 'tractors'.

Next, ask the children to get out from under the parachute, then lower it and place the four pieces of white fabric on top. Explain that these are the sheep in a field and that you need to chase them back to the farmer. Choose a farmer to walk around the edge of the parachute, then shake the parachute vigorously to throw the fabric squares out of it and invite the farmer to collect them.

Finally, tape brown ribbons as cows' tails to the backs of four children. Hold the parachute high as they crawl around underneath, and invite another farmer to try to catch their tails. Finish by lying on the parachute and singing your favourite farm nursery songs.

Support and extension

Encourage younger children to run one at a time under the parachute to collect just one egg. Ask older children to get a specified number of eggs, saying, for example, 'Elle, please collect three eggs'.

Home partnership

Create a booklet of favourite farm nursery songs and leave it in the book corner for parents and carers to share with their children.

Further ideas

♦ Hang sheets of fabric from a washing line and encourage the children to move between the sheets or crawl under the fabric.
♦ Chalk a track on the floor outside and encourage the children to run or to ride bikes or scooters along the track.

Theme links
Animals
On the farm

Jump aboard my caravan

Group size
Up to eight children.

What you need
Brochures and magazines about caravans; pictures of different travellers; two small rings or quoits; length of ribbon, approximately 6m long.

Preparation
Tie the ends of the length of ribbon together.

What to do
Look at the pictures of travellers and talk about their homes. Discuss with the children how it might feel to be a traveller, the excitement of new places, the sadness of leaving friends behind, travelling with family and friends and so on. Be careful to avoid stereotypes of travellers and encourage the children to think positively about different homes and life choices.

Now, look at the caravan pictures and talk about holiday homes. Invite the children to contribute their experiences and ideas. Arrange the length of ribbon on the floor to form a long narrow rectangle. Ask the children to stand inside it, one behind the other, and to hold the ribbon in one hand. Give the child at the front and the child at the back two small rings or quoits, one for each arm, to be the wheels of the caravan.

Invite the children to step forward very carefully, moving their caravan slowly. Then start to tell a simple story about a journey in a caravan, helping the children to move together in their imaginary one, over bridges, ducking under tunnels, up imaginary hills and so on. Ask them to contribute their own ideas about where they are going. End the journey with the children going to sleep in their caravan.

Support and extension
For younger children, play with just two children, using hoops instead of quoits. Plan the journey with older children, helping them to choose their own imaginary destination.

Home partnership
Ask parents and carers to collect pictures and photographs of caravans from holiday brochures. Encourage them to play games with their children, such as 'Skittles'.

Further ideas
♦ Arrange a visit to a caravan. Explore it together, looking at the different areas for cooking, sleeping, eating and so on.
♦ Make your own caravan play area, for example, throw a blanket over a climbing frame and add windows, a door, cooking utensils, dolls and a sleeping area.

Theme links
Holidays
Journeys and transport

I live above a shop

Group size
Two or three children.

What you need
Two cardboard boxes of the same size; wallpaper; scissors; glue; collage materials; small boxes and other recyclable materials; play people; doll's house furniture; tissue paper; dried pasta shapes; small lids; buttons; sticky labels; thin card; coloured pens.

Preparation
Take the children for a walk to the local shops and identify together which ones have flats above.

What to do
Talk with the children about the different shops and flats that you have seen. Discuss what it might be like to live in a flat above a shop.

Next, help the children to line the two boxes with paper, one for the 'flat' and one for the 'shop'. Decide what sort of shop you are going to make, then create a shop sign using pictures and words. Tape the two boxes together so that the flat is over the shop.

Now help the children to place the doll's house furniture in the flat and to use collage materials for the floor in different areas of the flat as well as to make items for the shop. Then make counters and drawers with the small boxes, and use the tissue paper to make fruit to sell, the buttons as pretend money and so on. Write prices on tiny bits of the sticky labels and add an 'Open'/'Closed' sign. Play alongside the children, commenting on what is happening and asking open questions. Help them to develop their own ideas and scenarios, adding more props as needed.

Support and extension
Prompt simple pretend play for younger children, modelling appropriate phrases, such as, 'Three apples, please'. Invite older children to make shopping lists for their customers.

Home partnership
Invite a parent who lives in a flat above a shop to come in to talk to the children about their life in the flat.

Further ideas
♦ Create a list of different types of homes, such as a flat, a terraced house, a bungalow and so on, and take the children for a walk to try to find some of them in your local area.
♦ Make two doors from large sheets of card, each with a home number, knocker and letter box. Turn these into entrances to the home corner and let the children play at being neighbours.

Theme links
My town
Shops

Watch out, little piggy!

Group size
Up to six children.

What you need
Three pieces of card; brown paint; sponges; cream or brown raffia; string; small twigs; glue; scissors; four paper plates; collage materials; hole-punch; ribbon; musical instruments.

Preparation
Familiarise yourself with the story 'The Three Little Pigs' (Traditional).

What to do
Tell the story of 'The Three Little Pigs' to the children and help them to draw the outline of a house on each piece of card, then carefully cut them out. Sponge-paint a brick effect on the first house, stick twigs on to the second house to create a house of sticks, and glue raffia and string to make a house of straw. Help the children to create collages of the faces of the three little pigs and the wolf on the four paper plates. Punch holes in the top of the plates and thread the ribbon through to make a handle for the children to hold the plates.

Now, with the children's help, retell the story, using the houses and character faces as props. Talk about how the animals are feeling. Ask the children to choose an instrument to represent each animal, then go back over the story using the props and the musical instruments. Gradually stand back and invite the children to add their own ideas, asking open questions to encourage them to develop their play.

Support and extension
Encourage younger children to join in with the 'huff' and 'puff' to blow the houses down. Help older children to extend their play into the home corner, adding dressing-up clothes and other props.

Home partnership
Write out a list of traditional tales that you share with the children in your setting and encourage parents and carers to read these stories with their children at home.

Further ideas
♦ Develop some story boxes for the children to share. Include a story-book, some objects from the story and a simple game. Allow the children to each choose a story box to share with another child in the book corner.
♦ Read *Moving Molly* by Shirley Hughes (Red Fox). Put a 'For sale' sign on your doll's house and add small boxes and a lorry next to it for removals.

Theme links
Animals
Traditional stories

Circle time

Circle time activities are designed for the whole group,
providing opportunities for the children to interact and to work
as part of a team. The activities increase the children's ability
to communicate effectively and to learn to share tasks.

In my home

What to do
Invite the whole group to sit in a large circle on a carpeted area, then take your place among the children.

Show the children the box or basket of objects. Choose an item and ask them to tell you about it, what it is and what it is used for. Encourage them to describe the object and say where it might be kept or used at home.

Next, pass the basket around the circle, inviting each child to choose an object and tell the rest of the group what it is, what it is for and so on. Ask open-ended questions and make comments to encourage each child to contribute. Ensure that all the children understand that this is a time for looking, listening and thinking, and that they should not interrupt another child.

Stepping Stone
Build up vocabulary that reflects the breadth of their experiences.

Early Learning Goal
Extend their vocabulary, exploring the meanings and sounds of new words.

Finish the session by choosing three or more objects from the basket and singing the song 'Here We Go Round the Mulberry Bush' (Traditional), using each object as a prop for a verse. For example, if you have selected a flannel, a wooden spoon and a watering can, the verses would be:

This is the way we wash our face, wash our face, wash our face,
This is the way we wash our face, on a cold and frosty morning.

This is the way we cook our dinner, cook our dinner, cook our dinner,
This is the way we cook our dinner, on a cold and frosty morning.

This is the way we water our plants, water our plants, water our plants,
This is the way we water our plants, on a cold and frosty morning.

Further ideas
♦ Make a display of objects used in different areas of a home. Encourage the children to bring in items from home and add them to the display.
♦ Place new items in the home area to extend the play, for example, baking trays, pretend food, weighing scales and cookery books to the kitchen area, or dolls for bathing, towels, shampoo bottles and so on for a bathroom (screen off a small area of the home corner to create one).

In Teddy's house

What you need
Small collection of teddy bears; very large sheet of paper; felt-tipped pens; easel or frame.

Preparation
Draw the outline of a simple house shape on the paper, then add different rooms, such as a kitchen, bathroom, living room and bedrooms. Draw a piece of furniture in each room that will help the children to identify the room, such as a cot for a baby room, a cooker in the kitchen, and so on. Attach the paper to an easel.

What to do
Invite the whole group to sit in a large circle on a carpeted area, then take your place among the children. Position the easel next to you.

Introduce the bears to the children and tell them about the house that you have drawn, talking about the different rooms. Pass each of the bears around the circle for each child to hold and say 'Hello' to.

Next, choose a bear and explain to the children that he is tired. Ask them what he might need. Prompt the children to tell you where he will sleep, what he needs to keep warm and so on, then invite a child to draw the items in the room, such as a blanket on to the bed, a cup next to it and so on. Let the child come to you to draw the item and then return to their place in the circle.

Continue playing the game, imagining, for example, that one bear feels hungry, one is cold, one is getting ready for nursery, one wants to have a story and so on. Ask the children for their ideas about how each bear feels and what it needs.

Finally, give a teddy to each child and encourage them to join in the action rhyme 'Teddy Bear, Teddy Bear, Touch Your Nose' (Traditional). Ask each child, in turn, to quietly pass their bear to another child, repeating the rhyme until all the children have had a turn.

Further ideas
♦ Use four large cardboard boxes fastened together side by side and ask the children to make a home for the bears, using blankets for beds in the bedroom, pots and pans for the kitchen, books, toys and a toy telephone for the living room, and a flannel, baby bath and towels for the bathroom.
♦ Sing 'There Were Ten in the Bed' (Traditional) with the children, using the teddy bears and a blanket for the props.

Home numbers

Stepping Stone
Show curiosity about numbers by offering comments or asking questions.

Early Learning Goal
Recognise numerals 1 to 9.

What you need
Objects from home showing numerals, such as a toy telephone, telephone directory, TV guide, catalogue, picture of a front door with a house number, calendar, calculator, birthday badge or card, story-books, clock; clothes with age label; pictures and photographs of these objects taken from books, newspapers and catalogues; list of all the children's first names on a large sheet of paper; marker pen; easel.

What to do

Invite the whole group to sit in a large circle on a carpeted area, then take your place among the children. Place the list on the easel and position it close to you.

Start by showing the children the different objects and pictures and spreading them out in the middle of the circle. Then ask each child, in turn, if their home has a number, and record each home number on the large sheet of paper, next to the child's name. If the child does not have a house number, let them choose one.

Now, ask each child to choose one of the objects and the corresponding pictures and to talk to the rest of the group about the object and describe its purpose. Encourage them to say if they have that object at home and in which room. Then ask them if there are other objects with numbers in that room and, if so, to name them. Prompt the child to name or point to some of the numerals on the picture or the object, or both.

Continue the game, giving each child plenty of time to select an object and talk about it. Encourage the rest of the group to listen carefully and to wait for their turn.

Finish the activity by writing four numbers on the large sheet of paper. Carefully dial this number on the toy telephone and pretend to talk. Then invite each child, in turn, to dial a number and 'chat' to their family or a friend on the telephone.

End circle time by singing a favourite number rhyme, such as 'Ten Fat Sausages' or 'One, Two, Three, Four, Five, Once I Caught a Fish Alive' (both Traditional).

Further ideas

♦ Add a list of telephone numbers and pictures next to the telephone in the home corner, such as a picture of a doctor and a number next to it.
♦ Use plastic numerals in wet sand, or tools such as spatulas and lolly sticks to draw the numerals.

Ssh, be gentle

Stepping Stone
Show care and concern for others, for living things and the environment.

Early Learning Goal
Understand what is right, what is wrong, and why.

What you need
A tiny soft-toy animal, such as a puppy or kitten; small basket or box; blanket.

What to do

Ask the children to sit in a large circle on a carpeted area, then take your place among them. Introduce them to the puppy or kitten and explain that he is very young, that your setting is strange and new to him, and that he needs a name.

Invite each child, in turn, to tell you if they have a pet at home and, if so, what it is called. If they do not have a pet, encourage them to tell you about a pet belonging to a friend or neighbour, or about a pet that they might like to have one day. Give each child an opportunity to hold the puppy or kitten in the basket, stroke him gently and then pass the basket carefully to the child sitting next to them.

Next, encourage the children to tell you how they think the puppy might be feeling, all alone in this new place. Take some of their suggestions and ask them what you might do to help the puppy. For example, he might be missing his mother, or he may be tired, hungry or frightened – what should you do in such cases? Talk about his needs and about why he might be feeling like that.

End circle time by asking each child to choose a name for the puppy.

Further ideas

♦ Set up an animal hospital with soft toys, bandages, plastic syringes, plastic medicine bottles, baskets and blankets. Also include a telephone, a diary for making appointments, pens and a notepad for writing prescriptions.
Ask a parent to bring their pet to your setting and to talk to the children about how they look after their it.
♦ Invite the children to make a 'This is where my pet lives' book. Encourage them to bring in photographs of their pets and make drawings of their homes, such as baskets, kennels, hutches or tanks, to add to the book. Display the book alongside story-books, picture books and information books about animal homes, pets and how to look after them.

Displays

This section gives suggestions for four specific interactive displays, each focusing on one of the 'Homes' mini themes developed in the activity chapters.

Magic machines

What to do

Help the children to select and cut out pictures of machines found in homes, then use the recyclable and collage materials to make models of these.

Line the display area with backing paper and make a border around it using grey and white paint. Then ask the children to paint vertical stripes on to the black paper border, bar-code style, and place the border across the backing paper. Cover the low table with bubble wrap and place the house at the centre of the back of the table. Attach the pictures and models on to the backing paper and make a line with the string from each object to the house, fixing it with glue, to create a web effect. Label each machine and place real familiar machines from homes, as well as books about them, on to the table for the children to explore.

Stepping Stone
Show an interest in ICT.

Early Learning Goal
Find out about and identify the uses of everyday technology.

Using the display

♦ Use Post-it notes and pens to make pretend text messages on toy mobile phones.
♦ Record the sounds that familiar machines make on to a tape recorder. Discuss these sounds and list the words that the children use. Then make a 'Noisy machines' rhyme, such as 'Click, click, tap, tap, rattle, ring', and add it to the display.

My street

Stepping Stone
Begin to construct, stacking blocks vertically and horizontally and making enclosures and creating spaces.

Early Learning Goal
Explore colour, texture, shape, form and space in two or three dimensions.

What you need
Wallpaper; low table or bench; recyclable model and collage materials; scissors; glue; paint; paintbrushes; pens; plastic bricks; shoeboxes; large cardboard box; doll's house furniture; play people; toy cars.

What to do
Invite each child to make a model of their home using a range of paint, pens together with collage and recyclable model materials and a shoebox. Focus on the shapes, colours and textures of the homes. Talk about other local buildings, such as shops, the library, schools and so on, and encourage the children to think about the colours, shapes and textures that they can see in these buildings. Work together to build models of some of these community buildings.

Next, place the table or bench against the display wall and ask the children to help you to cut the wallpaper to make a suitable backing for the street-scene display and to cover the table-top. Mount the buildings on to the wall at child level, resting them on the table-top, and leave a space large enough for the large cardboard box to be added next to these.

Invite the children to use the big box to make a doll's house, the lids being the front opening of the house. Paint or line the interior of the box with wallpaper and add the doll's house furniture and play people. Mount the box in the street scene, ensuring that the children can reach it easily. Make a road on the rest of the table, adding more buildings, cars and traffic-lights made from plastic bricks.

Using the display
♦ Add house numbers, street names and signs, drawn or cut from magazines.
♦ Make a post-box and tiny letters and postcards to post into the houses.
♦ Take photographs of local streets and buildings, ask the children to make drawings and paintings of houses and buildings, and combine them all to make an 'Our street' book.
♦ Print a border using sponges and polystyrene pieces to make a brick effect. Ask the children to draw the people who live in their homes, cut these out and mount them individually on the border.
♦ Look at a map of the local area and find the street names where the children live.

Nests and burrows

What you need
Green and blue backing paper; four sheets of A4 thin card; glue; staple gun (adult use); cardboard; scissors; small shoebox; plastic box; brown fabric; green Cellophane; paper; selection of painting, printing and collage materials; leaves and twigs; books about animal homes; pictures of an owl, beetle, frog and rabbit; soft-toy badger or mole; small toys; pictures of animals and fish that live underwater.

What to do
Look through the books of animal homes and discuss the different types of homes, such as nests, burrows, tunnels. Talk about which animals live on land, in water, or both.

Fix the green and blue backing paper on to your display wall. Ask the children to work together to decorate each sheet of card with the painting, printing and collage materials, so that they appear to be the bark of a tree, leaves on a woodland floor, the surface of a pond and a grassy bank. Fix one end of each card to the display so that the other end can lift like a flap, and under each card place a picture of an owl, a beetle, frog and rabbit respectively.

Cut a peep-hole in the long side of the shoebox. Mount the box low on the display board by stapling it from the inside with the peep-hole facing the children. Build a nest in the box with leaves and twigs, and place cardboard cut-out eggs into it. Let the children peek through the peephole to see if the 'eggs' have 'hatched'.

Now place the plastic box on its side, fill it with leaves and twigs, and add the soft-toy badger or mole. Cover it almost completely with brown fabric so that the children can just see its face with the rest of its body hiding in its 'burrow'.

Finally, add paintings of animals and fish that live in water to the blue area of the display, then cover this with strips of green Cellophane.

Using the display
♦ Use thick card, balsa wood and strong glue to build bird-boxes.
♦ Talk about pet fish and what they need in their home to be healthy.
♦ Dig a hole in the outdoor area and try to find minibeasts, and talk about animals that live in the garden or the park.
♦ Ask the children about their pets and where they live in their homes. Discuss what they need to keep warm, what they eat and where they sleep.
♦ Make some leaf prints and add them to the display.

Tall buildings

What you need
Corrugated card; small and large plastic bricks; six shoeboxes; string; cardboard tubes; staple gun (adult use); large matchbox; strong sticky tape; play people; doll's house furniture; collage and painting materials; sticky labels; pens.

What to do
Looking at pictures of tall buildings. Talk to the children about these and how people reach the top floor, for example, using the stairs or a lift, and how objects might be brought down, such as by a lift or down a chute.

Next, fix the corrugated card as backing paper on to the display wall, down to floor level, and explain to the children that you are going to make some very tall buildings. Ask them to paint and decorate each shoebox as a flat. Then cut a square hole, approximately 10cm x 10cm, in the side of each box for stairs to come

through and mount the finished boxes, one above the other, to make a tower block. Help the children to decorate and furnish the flats with the doll's house furniture. Build stairs with the small bricks from one flat to the other and add the play people. Use the large bricks to build other towers and tall buildings, and place these alongside the block of flats. Encourage each child to add their name to their flat or tower, using sticky labels and pens.

Now build the lift. Thread a length of string through a cardboard tube and fix the tube to the display board at the top of the flats with a staple at each end. Thread the string around a second tube that has been fixed next to the bottom of the flats. Tie the ends of the string together to form a continuous loop that acts as a pulley between the two card tubes, then attach a large matchbox to the string with strong sticky tape. Use this 'lift' to take play people up and down the tower block.

Using the display
♦ Measure the height of the buildings and find other objects that are the same height.
♦ Visit tall local buildings and ask the children to bring in pictures of tall buildings, flats, office blocks and churches.
♦ Use a piece of tube or plastic pipe to make a rubbish chute from the top of the flats and remove the rubbish with a toy lorry.
♦ Make a similar pulley arrangement with string and yoghurt pots in the sand or water tray.

Rhymes

Ouch! It's hot!

Grills and ovens cook our food
We need them very hot
But never, never touch them
As they will hurt a lot!

Radiators heat our homes
But they are hot to touch
So do not stand too close to them
As burns can hurt so much!

Our blazing fires look lovely
They keep us warm as toast
But never play near burning flames
As they can hurt the most!

Brenda Williams

House doors

Red, yellow, blue and green
Every house door to be seen.

One, two, three or four
Different numbers on each door.

Knocker, handle, letter box
Gold or silver coloured locks.

Every house a different key
Open up – what do you see?

Big or tiny, low or tall
Most doors open to a hall.

Carpet, cupboard, rising stairs
Telephone, lamp and wooden chairs.

This house here belongs to me
Let me tell you what I see...

*(Invite individual children to repeat the last
verse and name one object that they see inside
their front door.)*

Brenda Williams

Click, click, click
(Count each number on fingers.)

One for computer
Two for a switch
Three for a mouse
And a click, click, click.

Four for the program
Played on the screen
Five for the colours
Of red, blue, green.

Six for the printer
Click, click, click
Out come the pictures
Quick, quick, quick.

Seven for the laughter
Eight for the fun
Nine for the children
When the game is done!

Brenda Williams

Friends and neighbours

Friends and neighbours often meet
In the houses down our street.

Mrs Jones at number four
Has a yellow painted door.

Mr Smith next door to me
Has a house called 'Home From Sea'.

Auntie Jane from her high flat
Pops in our house for a chat.

But when we visit Auntie Flo
She lives in a bungalow.

Houses tall or houses small,
Friendly neighbours in them all.

Brenda Williams

Foundation
Themes
Homes

A house of patterns

Patterns on the windows, patterns on the doors
Patterns on the roof-tops, patterns on the floors.

Stained-glass windows, colours bright
Glass-door patterns, shape the light
Roof-top tiles of squares in line
Wooden floors of patterned pine.

Patterns on the brickwork, patterns on the drive
Patterns on the porch step, welcome you inside.

Brickwork patterns, build the wall
Driveway cobblestones, big and small
Mosaic porch with shapes which gleam
A house of patterns to be seen!

Brenda Williams

Spider, spider, spins all day

(Place the children in a circle [web], with one child acting as a spider in the middle.)

Spider, spider,　　　　　*(spider runs back and forth across the circle*
Spins all day　　　　　　*touching different children)*
Weaving his web
The spider's way.

Spinning them big　　　　*(web of children opens up wide,*
Spinning them small　　　*then closes in towards the centre)*
Spider, spider,
Spins them all.　　　　　*(spider looks pleased with himself)*

Webs are wide　　　　　*(web of children opens up wide,*
And webs are thin　　　　*then closes in towards the centre)*
But spider, spider,
Lives within.　　　　　　*(spider sits down in the middle of the web)*

Brenda Williams

Songs

When I'm going up (down) the stairs
(Tune: 'Yankee Doodle')

When I'm going up (down) the stairs,
I play a little game.
I count each step and do not stop
Until I reach the top (bottom).

The bottom step (first step down) is number one
And after that comes two.
Then three and four, five six and seven
Eight and nine and ten.

Sanchia Sewell

My wheelbarrow
(Tune: 'The Animals Went in Two by Two')

I pick up bricks and load them in my wheelbarrow *(x2)*,
I load the bricks up one by one, and when the loading up is done, I
Push my wheelbarrow wherever it needs to go.

I'm always careful as I push my wheelbarrow *(x2)*,
And even if the bricks are many, I take my time and don't spill any, I
Push my wheelbarrow wherever it needs to go.

To unload the bricks I tip them out my wheelbarrow *(x2)*,
And so you see my job is done, it really has been jolly good fun as I
Push my wheelbarrow wherever it needs to go.

Sanchia Sewell

The postie's bag

(Tune: 'Incy Wincy Spider')

Look inside the postie's bag and tell me what you see.
Lots and lots of letters, as many as can be.
Brightly coloured postcards with writing on the back,
And that is what you find in a postie's heavy sack.

Different types of leaflets advertising things.
Packages and parcels neatly tied with strings.
All the post for each house in a special pack,
And that is what you find in a postie's heavy sack.

Sanchia Sewell

Kitchen song

(Tune: 'She'll Be Coming Round the Mountain')

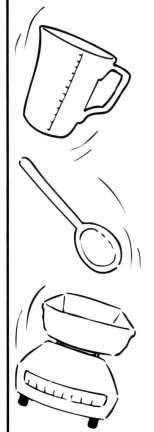

There's a cooker in our kitchen that is hot *(x2)*,
So we have to ask a grown-up, have to ask a grown-up,
Have to ask a grown-up for their help.

We can measure liquids in a measuring jug *(x2)*,
There are numbers that can tell us, numbers that can tell us,
Tell us how much liquid is inside.

We can weigh ingredients on a weighing scale *(x2)*,
There are numbers that will tell us, numbers that will tell us,
Tell us how much our ingredients weigh.

We make sure we leave the kitchen clean and tidy *(x2)*,
Though it's been a little messy, been a little messy,
We always leave the kitchen clean and tidy.

Sanchia Sewell

I wake up at seven o'clock

(Tune: 'Hickory Dickory Dock')

I wake up at seven o'clock
And get out of bed with a hop.
I dress myself from top to toe,
Then downstairs to breakfast I go.

I eat until I've had enough,
Then give my teeth a good brush.
I'm ready to start a brand new day,
I'm ready to have a good play.

At 12 it is time for some lunch,
Some sandwiches I can munch.
And then my friends come round to play,
I'm having a wonderful day.

And now it's the end of the day,
My toys have been tidied away.
I've had my bath, I've had my tea,
It's time to say night-night to me.

Sanchia Sewell

See that tall building

(Tune: 'Hey Diddle Diddle')

See that tall building that's got lots of windows
That stretches up to the sky.
The people that live on those uppermost floors
Don't have gardens, but only sky.

There is a number for every floor
From the bottom to the top.
And there is a number for every home
That this very tall building has got.

Sanchia Sewell

Paper house

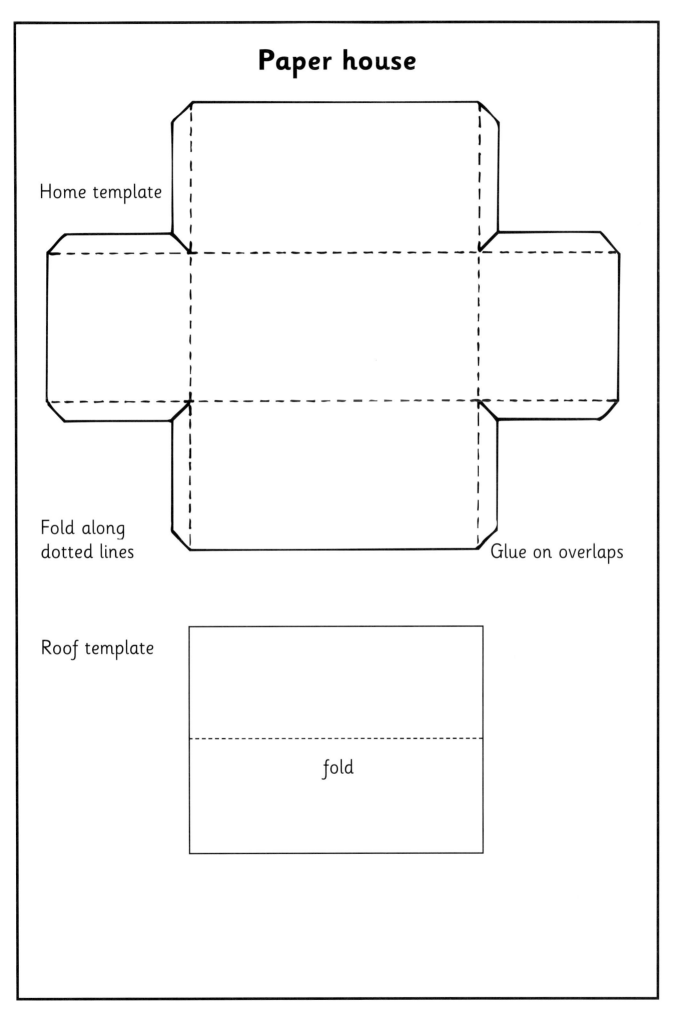

Home template

Fold along
dotted lines

Glue on overlaps

Roof template

fold

Zigzag book

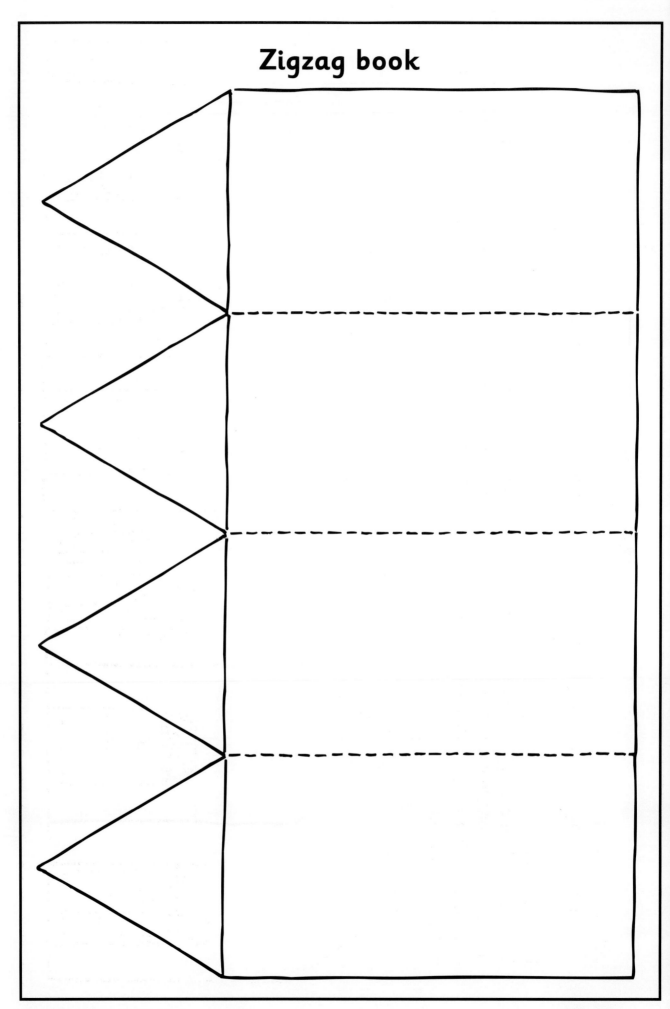

Where I live

What you need
A copy of this page for each child; dice numbered 1–6; small counters or buttons.

How to play
Give each child a copy of the board and invite the children to take turns to throw the dice and place a counter on the corresponding number on the house. Start with the youngest child. If the player already has a counter on that number, they must have another turn. Continue playing until all the houses on each child's board have a counter.

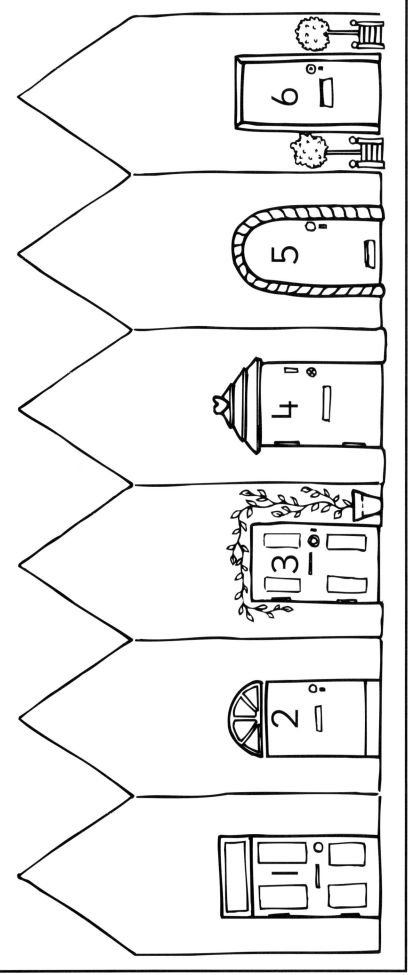

My routine

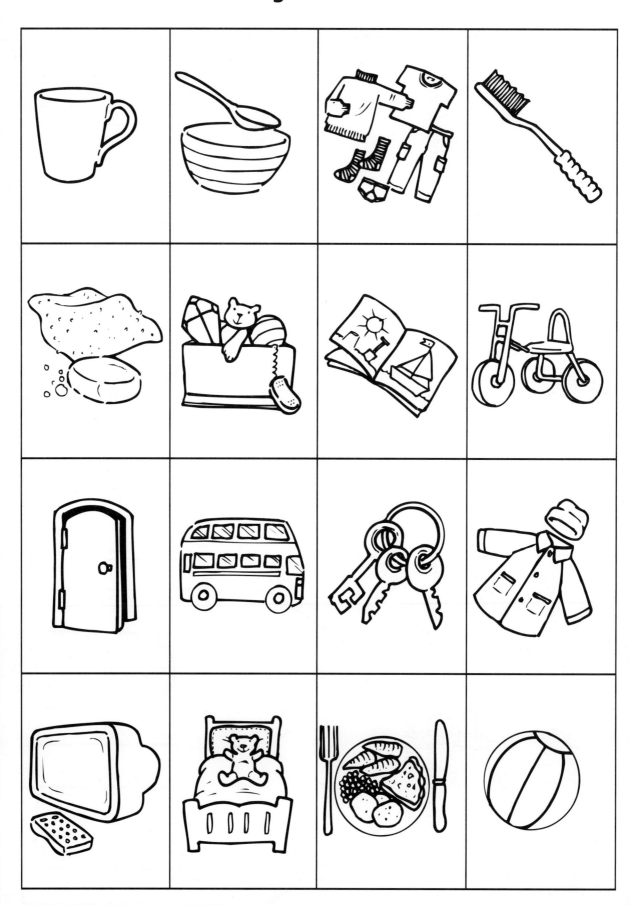

Gingerbread houses

250g plain flour

100g soft margarine

100g soft brown sugar

1 tbsp black treacle

1 tbsp golden syrup

1 tbsp orange juice

1 tbsp ground ginger

What you need
Large mixing bowl; kitchen scales; tablespoon; wooden spoons; rolling-pins; baking sheet; children's knives; plastic ruler; small tubes of coloured icing; small sweets; cake decorations.

What to do
Wash your hands!

Spoon the plain flour into the mixing bowl and rub in the soft margarine until the mixture looks like fine breadcrumbs.

Add the brown sugar, black treacle, orange juice and golden syrup. Next, add the ground ginger, then mix everything well.

Share the mixture out between the children and knead the dough well.

Scatter a little flour on to the table and help each child to roll out their dough mixture. Use the plastic ruler and children's knives to carefully cut out a house shape.

Bake the gingerbread houses for ten minutes at 180°C/350°F (Gas Mark 4).

Leave to cool, then decorate with icing, small sweets and cake decorations. Enjoy sharing the gingerbread houses!

Tickets and bookmarks

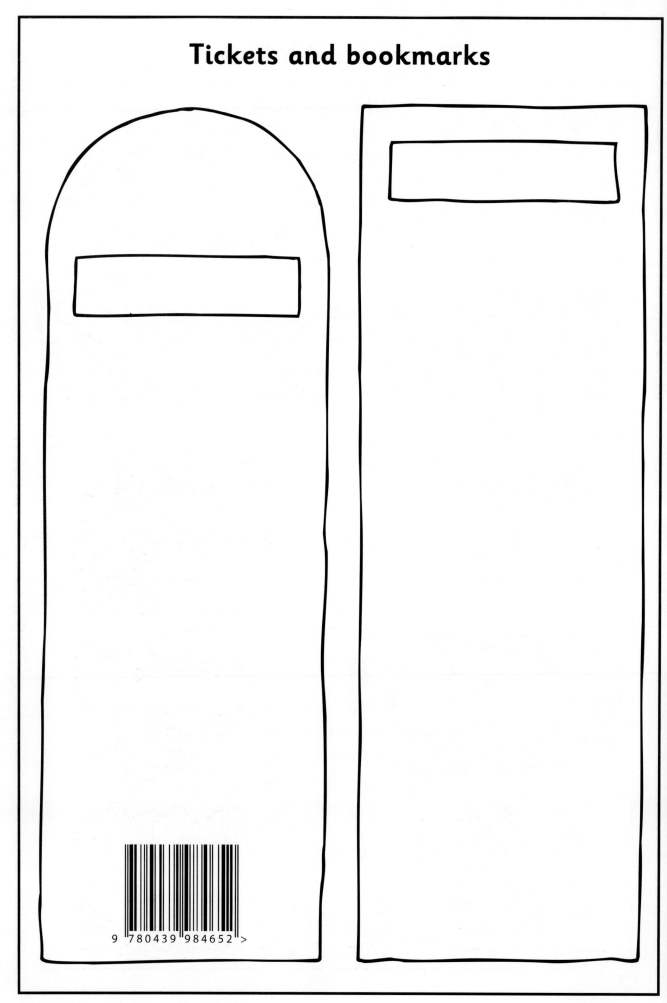

■SCHOLASTIC **Photocopiable**

Animal cards

House game

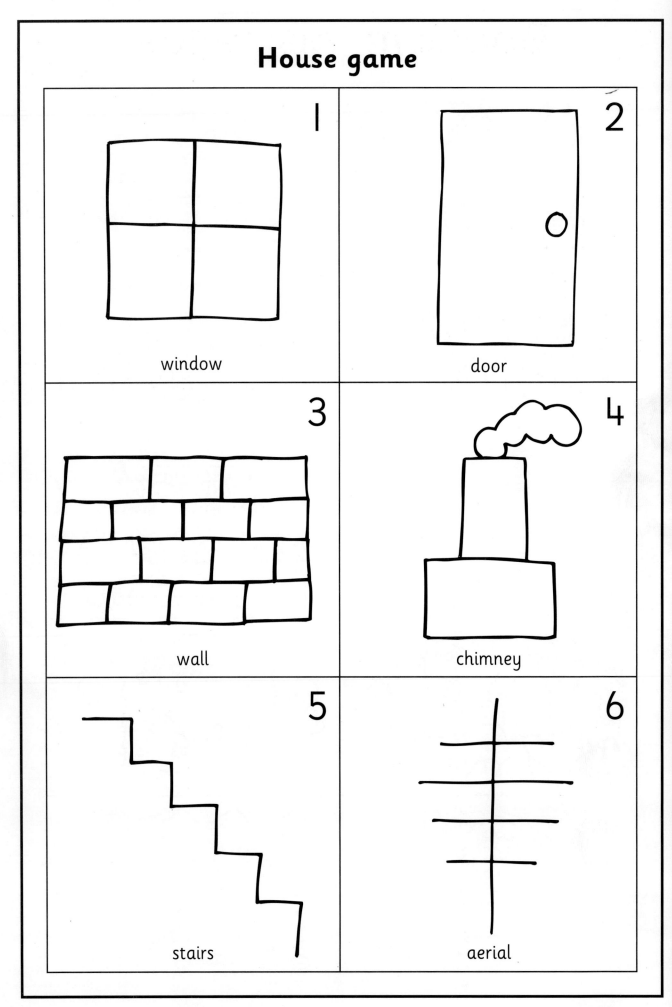

1 window

2 door

3 wall

4 chimney

5 stairs

6 aerial